The Great Bicycle Expedition

Books by William C. Anderson

The Great Bicycle Expedition

*Freewheeling through Europe
with a Family, a Potted Plant—
and Bicycleseatus*

BY WILLIAM C. ANDERSON

Crown Publishers, Inc., New York

Library of Congress Catalog Card Number: 73–82321
ISBN: 0-517-505975

Printed in the United States of America

Published simultaneously in Canada by General Publishing Company
Limited

Designed by Shari de Miskey

TO CHARLOTTE AND OTTO
WITH LOVE

"Bicycling isn't much like anything else. It has its similarities with walking and running and even with mountaineering, but as a sport it's unique. The feeling and discipline of pedaling yourself on an incredibly efficient and simple machine one hundred miles isn't quite like any other. The even movements, the constant and controlled effort, and the skill of traveling under your own power constitutes about as satisfying a sport as any."

—Two-Wheel Travel

"Does the road wind up-hill all the way?
Yes, to the very end."

"Up-Hill" (Stanza 1)

Saddlesores

The Great Bicycle Expedition

1

"Bicycle across Europe! You Outta Your Skull?"

"JOHNSON'S Baby Powder. That's what I used. Sprinkled it in the crotch of my shorts."

I looked across the coffee table at the slender, wiry, seventy-year-old man. "You squished around with your shorts full of Johnson's Baby Powder?"

Bobby Walthour tried to overlook my ignorance. "You don't notice it at all. Not in chamois-lined shorts. Fact is, feels pretty good."

"Chamois-lined shorts? That's an item of haberdashery I'm more inclined to associate with ballet dancers than bike riders—"

"You ever ridden in a six-day bicycle race, Mr. Anderson?"

"As a matter of fact, I haven't."

"Try it some time. Six days of chafing your inner thighs on a pie-shaped piece of leather. You'd be amazed at the things bike riders have used to reduce the friction. I personally have tried axle grease, Vaseline, coconut oil, you name it. Fellow I knew even tried a preliminary heat with his shorts stuffed with Jello."

Dortha looked at Walthour in amazement. "Jello?"

"Strawberry, as I recall. Bad idea. Dripped down his legs, made a mess of the track. Had to halt the heat. The timer thought he'd ruptured himself." Walthour grinned. "Ah, those were the days."

"They must have been," I said, turning my attention to the huge book of clippings on the coffee table. "I never realized bike racing was such a national sport in the old days."

Dortha and I studied the newspaper items dating back through half a century. Bobby Walthour, Jr., had been given more coverage on his biking exploits than received today by most champions in the sporting world. The yellowed articles blazed with headlines extolling the biking prowess of the slender young man who had won the Amateur Bike Championship of America in 1921—and then had gone on to win six six-day bike races, finish second three times, and third, once. Obviously a favorite with sport cartoonists, he was the target of many a speedball pen, and was shown posing in pictures with luminaries of the era ranging from Calvin Coolidge to Jimmy Durante.

The last insert of the scrapbook was a full-color advertisement—one of the old Camel cigarette ads that used to be displayed on the pages of the Sunday funnies. In cartoon style it depicted young Walthour triumphing over incredible odds to emerge the winner of a grueling race. The final frame showed a victorious Bobby leaning against his racer and holding up a pack of Camels, saying, "A bicycle racer needs lots of endurance. Camels never hurt my lungs."

"So you smoked Camels?" I asked, amused.

Walthour chuckled. "Never smoked a cigarette in my life. That's why Camels never hurt my lungs."

I laughed. "Even in the old days Madison Avenue never let the facts interfere with a good commercial."

"Camels paid a nice hunk of change for that testimonial. And they sent me a case of cigarettes every month. Still got some in the attic. Smoke?"

"Not twenty-year-old Camels. But thanks." I pulled out a month-old Benson & Hedges and lit it. "Fascinating. I never dreamed bike racing was such a . . ."

"I guess there wasn't too much to do in the old days. But biking was a damned good sport. Still is."

"And it's an honor to have such a distinguished cyclist in our house," said Dortha.

Walthour smiled at the wife. "You're very kind, Mrs. Anderson. But I was an amateur compared to my dad. Never did reach his fame. The sports writers called him the world's greatest bike rider." The gray-haired man made headlines with his hands. " 'Bobby Walthour, the Dixie Flyer. The World Champion.' I never did quite measure up."

I patted the thick book of clippings. "I'd say Bobby Walthour, Junior, did a pretty good job of filling the old man's pedals."

"Well, I tried. I really did. But best I could do was win the bike amateur championship of America." He reached down for his shoes. "So you're really going to try bicycling through Europe?"

I threw a quick look in the direction of the kitchen, where Dortha had disappeared with dirty coffee cups. There was no crash of china. I breathed a sigh of relief. The hum of the dishwasher had evidently washed out Walthour's remark. "I think so. I haven't told the wife yet, but I'm thinking seriously of doing my next book on the new cyclemania that seems to have gripped the world."

"I envy you. Helluva good idea. Europe's a great place to bike."

"I also want to combine the trip with a visit to old haunts. It's been twenty years since I've been to Europe."

"Sure love to be going with you."

"Come along."

"Much as the thought intrigues me, can't do it. Gotta stay home and take care of my birds and cats. If I'm gone that long, my cats will take care of my birds."

"If you have a change of heart, you're more than welcome. We could use an experienced cyclist along."

He put on his cycling shoes and started lacing them up. "If you're going to get serious about long-distance cycling, get a pair of shoes like this." I watched him lace up the shoes with the metal instep that had been made for him in Europe. He had taken them off in deference to Dortha's kitchen linoleum. He stuck up his foot so I could see the sole. "This cleat gets a good grip on the bicycle pedal. No slippage. And of course you wouldn't be caught dead without toe straps."

"Certainly wouldn't," I said, showing I wasn't a complete novice to the cycling world. "I wouldn't be caught dead without toe straps on my shoes."

"The toe straps go on the bike pedal. Not on the shoes. Helps give you a rotary motion when you cycle. Makes you a single unit with your machine." He cocked gray eyebrows at me. "You done much cycling?"

"A little," I said, determined not to be trapped again. "I had a paper route in school—"

"I mean cycling. Like a hundred miles a day."

"A hundred miles—a day?"

"Not uncommon at all. I averaged a hundred miles a day crossing the U.S. one time. That included biking over the Rockies."

I cleared my throat. "I wasn't exactly figuring on a hundred—"

"You can do it in no time. Just takes a little conditioning. Build up to it." He glanced down at my midriff, which was draped decorously over the coffee table. "You'll be rid of that in no time."

I sucked up my stomach, exposing an ashtray I had been looking for. "The sedentary job of the writer does not exactly groom one to create a stir at Muscle Beach. But beneath this temporary touch of tallow lie the heart and muscle of a great athl——"

"As I say, get some chamois cycling shorts. They're good. Line them with several layers of smooth nylon. Really cuts down the friction. And remember, lots of Johnson's Baby Powder. Best ball bearings—pardon the expression—you can get."

"I'll certainly remember."

"If I were you I'd get a bike right now and start practicing. Every day. You and the missus. Then when you get to Europe you can start right off."

The cyclist gathered up his belongings, paid his respects to Dortha, and I walked him to his bike parked in the carport. "You ever ridden a ten-speed?" he asked, unlocking his bicycle.

"No."

"Right now's a good time. Just picked this bike up. Had it made in England."

"It's a beautiful thing. Must have cost a fortune."

"Got a bargain. Six hundred dollars. Has special gearing. For these hills around Lake Arrowhead."

I whistled. "That's a lot of bucks for a bike."

"Not necessarily. Some cost as much as a car. Hop on. Take a little spin."

My emphatic demurrals were ignored. No way was I going to get out of trying Walthour's new machine. Reluctantly I planted my buttocks on the seat, just to gratify my guest. I looked down the steep incline that led from the carport to the street below. "I don't think I'd better go down that hill."

"No problem. I just rode up it. That's a sneeze compared to what you'll find in Europe."

"This bike insured?"

He dismissed the thought with a wave of his hand. "Go on."

I went.

I shouldn't have.

As the bike picked up speed, I started to put back pressure on the pedals to brake. Instead of braking anything, the pedals spun as easily backward as they did forward. *"This thing's got no brakes!"* I yelled, a chuckhole opening a wide gap between seat and sitter.

Dimly I heard the voice from the Mount. *"They're on the handlebars!* THE HANDLEBARS!"

I reached for the handlebars.

But it was too late.

The collision did very little damage to the hundred-foot Ponderosa Pine that sheltered our access road. And except for miscellaneous cuts and bruises, it did little damage to me. But the injury to an expensive, handmade English bicycle with special gears was another story. There is not a big demand for racing bicycles with oval wheels.

I demanded to pay for it, but Walthour would have none of it. He insisted that the damage was minimal, that the spokes could be straightened, that the bike would soon be as good as new. Besides, he blamed himself for not checking me out on the bicycle before urging me to solo.

I felt like a Class A heel until several days later. Dortha and I were on the front deck of our A-frame enjoying a coffee break, when who should ride by but Bobby Walthour, Junior, dressed in cycling shorts, his muscular legs pumping calmly up the road. Under him was his English cycle, looking just like new.

"Look!" said Dortha. "Bob's got his bike fixed."

"I'll be damned." We hailed him. He stopped just long enough to return a friendly greeting, but refused a cup of coffee because he had a date in the village. With Freda Hoffmeir. She had just gotten a new ten-speed. Then he started down the road, shifting his gears in a fluid movement to accommodate the hilly terrain, his rotating cycling shoes sprinting him out of sight in no time.

"I don't believe it," said Dortha.

"I don't either. I made metal spaghetti out of that machine."

"I don't mean that. Freda Hoffmeir. She's seventy-five if she's a day!"

"Probably. But this bicycling business doesn't seem to have any age limits. I'd give my next royalty check to be able to wheel around like young Walthour. And he's in his seventies."

"He's an amazing man. I like him."

"Likewise. And I'm glad he's a new neighbor. He'll come in handy." I bit my tongue.

"Handy?" Dortha leveled her green eyes at me. "How handy, dear?"

This was not the time to tell her of my new book. I guided her back into the living room. "Just handy. I find that all neighbors are handy up here in the mountains. Don't you?"

I received a suspicious look. "Andy, you're not up to something?"

"You know better than that, dear."

It would be better to break the news tonight. During happy hour. I would ply her with Fresca and win her to a mellow mood. Then drop the bomb.

Dortha was a nice person. She was also the world's greatest housekeeper, a Picasso of the pantry, and one helluva roommate. But, as even the Hope diamond has a flaw—minuscule, to be sure—so does my wife. The redhead had been shortchanged;

she had the resiliency of a tombstone. She thrived on an immaculate, patterned, a place for everything and everything-in-
its-place existence. And any encroachment on this well-ordered
life-style was met with the subtle reception of a tigress at bay.

When I had told her, several years earlier, that we were
going across Canada on the new Trans-Canada Highway in a
travel trailer with two kids and various and sundry livestock
the offspring had labeled as pets, her tail twitched threaten-
ingly. When I told her we were going to sell our beautiful home
in Woodland Hills, California, and build our own mountain
A-frame in the San Bernardino National Forest while we lived
in it, low snarls issued through bared teeth. And when I told
her we were going to spend the summer busting up her routine
by cruising down the Mississippi River in a houseboat, I was
greeted by loud snarls and slashing claws.

To be sure, these reactions were short-lived. They lasted
only as long as it took her to develop a new routine, whether
bouncing along in the trailer, living in a house inhabited by
plumbers and carpenters, or rocking along in our headstrong
houseboat. Once her new patterns were established, her life
again orderly, she returned to her sweet, loving disposition.

But I did not look forward to the seismographic registra-
tions that always accompanied the first breaking of the news.
And a bicycle trip through Europe! How would she *ever* develop a nice, easygoing pattern when her flanks were envelop-
ing a bicycle seat the size of a pie slice, and her belongings
had to be carried in a suitcase strapped to her bicycle? I was in
for a siege.

As I headed toward my den, I noticed a clipping on the
floor that had evidently escaped Bobby Walthour's scrapbook.
Picking it up I saw it was a drawing from the old "Strange As
It May Seem" series. It depicted Bobby Walthour pedaling hell-
bent around a bicycle track. Under the drawing was the cap-
tion "Bobby Walthour—6-day bike champion in 1903—was pro-

nounced dead twice, 'fatally' injured 6 times, broke his right collarbone 28 times, his left collarbone 18 times, and had 32 fractured ribs. . . . He had more than 100 body scars from bruises and cuts, and 60 stitch scars on his face and head."

I looked around, saw I was unobserved, and surreptitiously stuffed the clipping into my pocket.

It was going to be tough enough as it was.

I mixed a double batch of liquid courage, capped the gin bottle, and dive-bombed my martini glass with two olives. I poured a Fresca for Big Red, sliced a hunk off a wheel of Gouda cheese, and got out the crackers. While accomplishing the latter I managed to stumble over the wife, who was in the process of being swallowed by the oven of the kitchen stove. There was a muffled oath.

"Time to get out of the oven, dear," I said. "The salubrious hour is at hand."

Dortha emerged from the stove, tossed cleaning rags into the sink, and collapsed on her haunches. She blew back a strand of hair from her eyes and said, "Hate this job. If I had a spouse who truly loved me, he'd buy me a self-cleaning oven."

"You're probably the only woman in the world who cleans the oven after every meal. Whether you use it or not. I'm gonna get you a job in a space laboratory. You can spend all day vacuuming your uniform."

"Oh, hardy har." She patted the kitchen floor beside her. "If you want to spend happy hour with me you'll have to sit here. I haven't the strength to move."

"I'm with you." I put the hors d'oeuvres on the floor at her feet, handed her her Fresca, and sank down beside her with my drink. "This sure beats that million-dollar view of the lake we have on the front deck. First time I've seen the underside of your chopping block."

"If you don't like it here, leave already."

"I like it. It means spending happy hour with my true love. Tomorrow, how about the furnace room?"

"It's a date." She touched her glass with mine. "I see we're drinking a double tonight. Thistles in the literary vineyards?"

"*Au contraire.* Luscious, plump grapes. Finished proofing the galleys of *Hurricane Hunters* and sent them off. Another Anderson novel is about to burst upon the publishing world with a cymbal crash of apathy and a bugle blare of ennui."

"That book should do very well."

"Maybe. Who knows what evil lurks in the minds of book reviewers? But let's talk about us, sexy lady."

"Let's do." She patted my cheek with a hand smelling of oven cleaner. "Perhaps I can seduce you with the heady smell of my Easy-Off."

"Later." I took a large pull from my drink, pondering just how to put it. "With my decks now cleared, I'm ready to embark upon my next venture."

"Wonderful. You're not still harboring thoughts about that crazy balloon idea? Going across Russia in a hot-air balloon?"

"No. The Russians shot my balloon idea down in flames."

"Not your pornographic book?"

I shook my head. "I doubt if the world's quite ready for the *Sordid Sex Secrets of Calvin Coolidge.*"

"You could be right. What then?"

I studied my olive. Dortha was already on the floor, pretty well beaten into submission by her domestic chores. This was probably as good a time as any. I drained my glass and threw caution to the winds. "I'm thinking, dear, of doing a book on bicycling. From first-hand experience."

She looked at me, her green eyes sparking. "A *bicycle* book?"

I eyeballed the distance to the chopping block and the menacing meat cleaver that hung from its side. Considering

Dortha's present state of exhaustion, I could probably intercept her before she reached it. "I thought we might take the whole family and bicycle across Europe."

I steeled myself for the explosion.

There was the sound of gurgling Fresca followed by a loud exclamation. "*Bicycle! Across Europe! The whole family!*"

I rose on the pretense of fixing another drink, positioning myself between mate and cleaver. "Yes."

"*You?* Who are still licking your wounds from your last bicycle ride?"

"Yes."

"Andy! That's a *fantastic* idea!"

I dropped the gin bottle. "What did you say?"

"A *marvelous* idea! I love bicycles. And biking is so popular now. Everybody's doing it. For ecology reasons, for physical exercise—and what a way to lose weight!" She scrambled to her feet and embraced me. "And you know how I've been wanting to go back to Europe. Andy, I love you!"

"This isn't exactly the response I anticipated. I mean you were somewhat less than enraptured about past ventures—"

"We can visit our old hangouts in Europe. Look up old friends. Do our Christmas shopping." She patted her stomach. "And I can get rid of my little pot you've been mumbling about. And we can take one more family trip with our college kids and see if we can cope with them as adults. And I can visit my brother's grave in Holland." She gave me a big kiss. "Andy, you are the dearest, sweetest, most wonderful husband in the whole wide world."

I didn't bother with olive, ice, or vermouth. Nor did I try to comprehend the unpredictability of women. I just poured a straight shot and gulped it down.

I was still reeling from the shock of unexpected acquiescence about the upcoming venture when Dortha surprised me with another. As much as we loved our beautiful mountain home shouldering the clouds atop the San Bernardino Mountains at Lake Arrowhead, it was becoming increasingly apparent that we had too much house for just the two of us. With both kids in college, we found ourselves wandering around the three-tiered, seven-decked monstrosity like a couple of Chloes, passing each other like ships in the night, embracing on chance meetings like two star-crossed lovers. Dortha was seldom seen divorced from mop, vacuum, or dustcloth, and my brow began to wear perma-pressed wrinkles from trying to keep ahead of the payments, maintenance, and heating bills.

For a long time nothing was said between us. We had hand-built this house with blood, sweat, and mortgages. It was to be our last home, the end of our frustrating bouts with movers. It was to be the shrine in which, when the time came, we would adjourn to the wine cellar—Dortha with her vacuum cleaner, I with my typewriter—to brick up the door and expire elegantly along with a case or two of chablis.

When I finally mustered the courage to tell the redhead that prudence might best be served by moving to smaller quarters, thereby reducing the area that had to be mopped, polished, and cleaned—not to mention painted, heated, and electrified—I was surprised to find she was just at the point of suggesting it herself. So with heavyhearted commiseration we decided the time was opportune—especially since we would be gone for several months—to put the house on the market. To ameliorate the pain of parting from a beloved old friend with the anticipation of departing on a grand trip.

The unexpected house sale with the quick escrow threw our plans into overdrive. Dortha bemoaned the fact she would not have time to properly clean the house (I never saw it when you couldn't perform open heart surgery on the kitchen floor without fear of infection), and she swept through it like Hurricane Agnes, shampooing rugs, cleaning drapes, waxing walls and floors.

Scott and Holly, coming home from college, quickly discovered they had made a mistake. There was no place they could hide from their mother, and they even went so far as to look for summer jobs to get out of the white tornado's vortex that involved such a plebeian pastime as household work. Unsuccessful at finding a job for such a short time, they were both soon caught up in the maelstrom that involved stepladders, paintbrushes, scrub buckets, and that most horrible nemesis of the long-haired set—manual labor.

I retired to my den sanctuary on the third floor, hoping to rise above the storm. But even here I was vulnerable, as I kept finding subtle hints like caulking guns on my typewriter, Windex and clean rags buried in my typing paper.

Hoping to follow Bobby Walthour's advice and get bicycles before we left so we could begin our pre-trip conditioning, I soon found our calendar wasn't long enough. By the time I had organized trips to Los Angeles for passports and inoculations, buttoned up my office, and packed all our belongings for storage, it was time to go to the bank for closing of the escrow.

This had allowed little time for research on biking, limited to a fast perusal of the *North American Bicycle Atlas* by Warren Asa and Dell's *Two Wheel Traveling: Bicycle Camping and Touring*. Both were fine publications, the former dealing, obviously, with North America and of limited use to our proposed European junket; the latter dealing with techniques of biking and camping, but containing only a brushover treatment of continental cycling. With the bicycle revival now encompassing over eighty-five million Americans of all ages, I unearthed several magazines devoted to the pastime—*Bicycling, Bike World, Bicycle Spokesman,* and *Two-Wheel Trip*—a beautiful effort published in San Francisco.

Our eager-to-please Lake Arrowhead librarian produced several books devoted to riding techniques, how to repair your bike, and hosteling on bicycles; other than this I found an amazing paucity of material devoted to a sport that witnessed the sale of no less than seven million bicycles last year alone. Maybe we were, indeed, plowing virginal journalistic ground with our proposed odyssey.

We had not decided on the make of bicycle to buy, as every expert I consulted had a different idea. With dozens of good brands of touring bikes on the market, the choice was extremely difficult. Bobby Walthour suggested I should settle for nothing less than a handmade, custom bike from England equipped with a special Alpine climbing gear. When apprised of the price—starting at $500—I multiplied this by four and speedily decided that an off-the-shelf model would be more in tune with our project, even if it meant *pushing* our bikes up the Alps. When I checked with the airlines and ascertained the prices involved in flying bikes across the Atlantic, I decided to pick up our equipment in Europe. Thereby not only saving a considerable freight bill, but also taking advantage of European experts who could better advise on the type of equipment best suited for our European conquest.

In order to establish mail-pickup points, it was essential that some type of itinerary be worked out. This involved purchase of a *Kummerly & Frey* European road map, which I nearly wore out before even starting the trip, trying to figure the distances a four-man cycling team could make in a day: a neat trick in itself considering none of the family had done any bicycle touring, no one was in especially good shape, and two of the party had not even touched a bicycle in a quarter of a century. Not counting my recent Kamikaze mission. Only Holly had checked out on a ten-speed, having bought one at college as a sop to a dedicated Phys. Ed. instructor who was determined to produce at least one bead of perspiration on each student before graduation. Cycling was Holly's P.E. elective, as it was the only sport offered she could do sitting down.

Finally, in desperation, I came up with a proposed route that would see us averaging some fifty miles a day through half a dozen countries, and selected several major cities as mail-pickup points. Seriously doubting we would ever arrive at any of them, I dispatched the itinerary to relatives, friends, my publisher, my agent, and a host of nervous creditors.

The time had come.

With the escrow closed, our household goods ensconced in storage, our suitcases packed and loaded in the Buick, we made one final check around the house. For the last time my misty-eyed wife filled the hummingbird feeder, emptied the last of the peanuts into the squirrel dish, and restocked the suet for the birds.

A solemn-faced crew climbed into the car. There was none of the levity that usually accompanied the start of a looked-forward-to journey. The kids had loved our home as much as we. They had shared in its building, become adults in its shelter. It was more than huge beams and split-cedar shingles. House had been a happening, a sanctuary, a sanctorum. It had been the pad for wall-to-wall sleeping bags occupied by the siblings' friends; the scene of great parties; a rendezvous for old buddies. It had been the subject of a successful book and might be the locale of a movie someday. Its timbers had shared the laughter of a happy family. It had soaked up a tear or two.

House had been a home in every sense of the word.

Dortha bade a quiet farewell to Fred and Sam, her favorite squirrels, then locked the door and secreted the key where the new owners could find it. Wordlessly she climbed into the car. I started up and headed down the access road. Turning on Matterhorn Drive I stopped in front of the house for one last look. House stared down at us reproachfully, its sparkling windows throwing back the early morning sun. The massive shoulders of its wings seemed to shrug in resignation.

I tugged the tissue box out of the glove compartment and passed it around as we proceeded down the road.

We said very little for a good many miles.

2

"A Good Bicycle Seat
Is Your Best Asset"

IT was our plan to drive across the States to New York, where we would catch our charter flight for Europe. The second night on the road we arrived at Boulder, Colorado, on schedule, to spend a couple days with Dortha's sister, Alice Pruett, and her husband, Fred. A couple of our favorite relatives, we always looked forward to seeing them.

Fred owned the Pruett Publishing Company in Boulder, and he and Alice had always taken a vicarious interest in our adventures, even going so far as to join us on occasion—such as on our houseboat trip down the Mississippi. As weekend cyclists they were giving serious thought to meeting us somewhere in Europe during our upcoming expedition.

At a party that evening, Fred said he had invited the Alleys. Hartley and Jean Alley, an interesting couple, were Boulder's contribution to the cycling world. I had read about the Alleys during my research, and knew they ran the highly acclaimed Touring Cyclist Shop, a mail-order house, from Boulder. Pruett warned they were a dignified, circumspect couple who were very nice people, but they took their cycling seriously and brooked no foolishness. I assured him I would be careful not to shake the family tree.

17

I was somewhat startled, therefore, when, in the midst of my bartending chores in the Pruett kitchen, I suddenly found myself goosed by a bicycle horn. I was further discomfited to find the bicycle horn was firmly attached to a bicycle, one of two that had just ridden into the kitchen. "What does a guy have to do around here to get a drink?" asked a ruddy-complexioned man with grinning teeth.

"For one thing, you gotta quit goosing the bartender." I held out my hand. "You must be Hartley Alley."

"I must be. Nobody else would claim a name like that." He gripped my hand. "This is my wife, Jean. I know you're Anderson. Pruett said you didn't like to migrate too far from the bar."

I shook hands with a charming woman who fairly oozed good humor and *joie de vivre*. "Very glad to meet you both," I said, meaning it. "Your reputation has preceded you."

"I was afraid of that," said Hartley, as they dismounted and secured their bikes. "We drinking Pruett's booze?"

"We are."

"Then we'll have a couple double Scotches. Apiece."

"Coming up." Quickly dispatching bartender duties, I presented them each with a large glass.

"Here's looking at you." Hartley started to toast, then put his drink down. He started fiddling with his glasses. "Guess I'd better take off my rearview mirror. I'm toasting not only you, but the gang in the room behind us."

I watched curiously as he removed a small mirror that extended from his glasses. "A rearview mirror on your spectacles?"

"Of course." Jean removed the mirror attached to her glasses. "Don't you use a rearview mirror when you cycle?"

"As a matter of fact, no. I didn't know there was such a thing."

"Good grief! And you're cycling through Europe? On

some of those roads? How are you going to know what's behind you?"

"I never figured that was a problem. Don't cyclists have the right of way?"

"In most countries," said Hartley, taking a large quaff from his drink. "But a lot of good your legal rights are going to do you when you're pushing up six feet of sod."

"You have a point." I made a mental note to get four rearview mirrors. "Those are mighty fine-looking bicycles," I said, appraising the low-slung touring bikes.

"We're happy with them."

"What kind of exotic European make are they? Or are they Japanese?"

Hartley grinned. "Would you believe they're made in Chicago? They're Schwinn Paramounts. Only top quality ten-speed made in the U.S. Notice the derailleur?"

"That's a nice-looking one," I said, wishing I knew what the hell the derailleur was.

"It's a Japanese Sun Tour. Installed them on both our bikes. I think it's the best derailleur made." Fortunately, Hartley pointed at a small S-shaped gadget slung under the rear bicycle gear. Through it the bicycle chain was threaded. "Handles a wide range. Fourteen to thirty-four teeth."

I figured the derailleur must be the device that changed gears by realigning the sprocket chain. "They're better than American-made derailleurs?"

Hartley took a swig from his drink. "No derailleurs made in America. Labor's too expensive. Good bike construction takes a lot of time and manual labor. That's why most good equipment is foreign made. Italy, France, Japan, and Spain."

"Fascinating."

"Frustrating. Ever tried to get a Japanese derailleur part in Clovis, New Mexico?"

"No."

"Forget it. Our only salvation is that the Japanese make pretty good bike equipment. Seldom breaks down."

I looked at Hartley with the awe of the shoeshine boy in the presence of Muhammad Ali. "I'll bet you've chalked up a good many miles on that machine."

"A few. Jean and I got hooked on cycling about ten years ago. Since then we've biked extensively through the U.S., Europe, and Mexico." He patted his bicycle seat. "Just about got my seat broken in."

I looked at the tiny, pear-shaped seat. "That's a seat? Looks like one of Mickey Rooney's ballet slippers." I felt it. Instead of being hard and stiff like the few bicycle seats I had seen, it was almost pliable.

"I always break in a new seat with neat's-foot oil. Rub it into the leather real good. Makes the leather soft and conform to your posterior. Minimizes chafing."

I slapped my ample caboose. "Do they make a bicycle with bucket seats?"

He surveyed me critically over the top of his glass. "I get the feeling you haven't done a lot of cycling, Andy."

I cleared my throat. "I had a bicycle route when I was a kid."

He choked on his drink. "And that's the sum total of your cycling experience?"

"Except for a recent instance I'd rather not discuss."

"And you're cycling through Europe?"

"I am," I said smugly, hitching my stomach up out of the canapé tray. "Any law that says you gotta be a Bobby Walthour to ride a bicycle?"

"I think I'd better have another drink." I administered to his needs. "I'm not knocking it. I think it's a great idea. But it might have been wise to do a little conditioning. Get into shape. How long do you have for your trip?"

"Couple months."

"Hmmmm. Too bad you're going to spend part of your trip seeing Europe on charley horses."

"I'd hoped to get some practice. But we unexpectedly sold the house and pushed up our departure time. So now we're just going to wing it. And I don't think that's all bad."

"Not bad. Just uncomfortable for awhile. Fred says you're a writer. Doing a book on the trip?"

"I am. The Anderson tribe has done a lot of wild things. A couple reviewers have tagged me the George Plimpton of the Geritol set. Last summer we took a houseboat down the Mississippi River. With absolutely no boating experience."

"So that's it. You got some kind of death wish."

"Not at all. I read a houseboat ad that said anyone could run a houseboat. I merely wanted to find out."

"You couldn't have found out without going down one of the most treacherous rivers in the world?"

"Probably. But I wanted to make an adventure out of it. The whole family did."

"I see. And that's how you're going to approach your bicycling-through-Europe book?"

"In a sense. Not only do I want to find out firsthand what is so exciting about the new bike craze that's sweeping the country, but I see in it another dimension. A great way to see the world. Too many people take a Tuesday-this-must-be-Liechtenstein tour, spend a week on a jet-propelled bus, touch the capitals of a dozen countries, then go back home broke, dead tired, confused, and unfulfilled. It's like visiting New York City, eyeballing the Statue of Liberty, and saying you've seen the United States. We want to *really see* Europe. Meet the Europeans. Stay in the small towns. In private homes when possible. Avoid the tourist traps. Meet someone besides hippies from California and newlyweds from New Jersey. Travel the back roads and the byways. That's where it's at. To me, every big city is the same. Here or in any other country. Congested, polluted, short-fused, and paved with dog dung. No, thank you."

Jean nodded her head and looked at her husband. "I understand what Andy's saying, Hartley."

Hartley flashed his palm. "Oh, I agree. I agree. There's no way in the world you can travel and have more eyeball contact with the natives than plowing through their grass roots on a bicycle. Don't get me wrong. I think it's a great idea." His eyes dropped to my solar plexus. "I only wish—unless you're wearing a thick money belt—you could have had time to get into shape."

I ignored the last remark. "I'm also exploring another aspect of foreign travel by bicycle. I think it can be done cheaply. Maybe cheap enough to bring it into the range of families or groups who have automatically rejected a trip abroad as being too expensive. Overseas charter flights are getting less costly all the time. And once in a foreign country it's pretty hard to find a cheaper conveyance than one that runs on excess flab. I could be very wrong, but I'm going to find out."

I noticed the first flickering look of approval in Hartley's eyes. "Pruett said you had the courage of your convictions. It was just your convictions he was worried about. Personally, I think you're going to have a ball. Once you get over your cramps, charley horses, and muscle spasms. You taking a sag wagon?"

"A sag wagon?"

"A jeep or small bus. Most touring groups use one. It carries the baggage, spare parts, and first-aid kit. Also picks up loose teeth, mangled bicycles, and people who just sag and can't go any farther. Hence the name, sag wagon."

"Interesting. But no. I don't think that would work for our small group. Besides being costly, it would mean one of us would have to drive the wagon. We all want to cycle."

"There'll be nasty days. Rain. Wind that blows you backward. You're not going to try to stick to any kind of itinerary?"

"A very loose one. I understand the European trains are very inexpensive and very good. If we get too far behind, or if bad weather socks in, we'll just hop a train and catch up."

Hartley mulled this. "Might work. Just might at that."

"Remember, we're going to see if this trip can be done economically. Within the range of the average American."

"More power to you. And it'll be very interesting to see how it all works out. Europe's no bargain basement anymore. Not like it used to be. You may find that Onassis couldn't afford the trip you're planning."

"Quite possible. Instead of a couple months, we may be heading back in a couple weeks."

"You can still cut corners. Live cheaply if you play your cards right. Plan to do any camping?"

"No. We've done the canteen and sleeping-bag bit. Having waged several lively campaigns with my family, I've found that low grumblings and mutinous threats from the troops generally dissolve in a hot shower and a warm bed. Besides, Big Red insists on it."

"No matter. If you stick to the back roads I think you'll find the little pensions and small hotels are comfortable and still inexpensive."

"I'll let you know in a couple months."

Hartley moved to the back of his bicycle. "What are you doing about panniers?"

I put a head on my drink while I tried to divine what a pannier might be. "I've been giving them a lot of thought. Got any suggestions?"

"Yes." He put his hand on a nylon pack slung over his rear bicycle wheel. "I got fed up one time on a long tour of Europe with the clumsy and inefficient panniers, so I designed my own." In a few seconds he had unhitched two handsome nylon bags from each side of his bike. He then zipped them together, attached a shoulder strap, and held up a very respectable looking piece of luggage. "The bags are eight-ounce waterproof rip-stop nylon." He demonstrated no fewer than ten compartments, beautifully designed—including one for shoes, and one that would accommodate a six-pack of beer.

"You've certainly thought of everything," I marveled, hoisting the extremely light piece of luggage.

"We handle them in our mail-order house. When you get your bikes, if you want several sets, we'll airmail them to you."

"Fine. I have no idea of the touring equipment available in Europe, but if we hit any snags you'll be the first to know."

"One other suggestion on packing. Everybody tries to take too much. Pack as little as you can. Then leave half of that at home. You'll be glad you did."

"Thanks, Hartley. I'll remember that."

"Do you plan on biking through France at all?"

"Northern France."

"Jean and I are taking an IBTS trip through Brittany and the Loire in late September. Maybe you'd like to join us for part of it?"

"What's an IBTS trip?"

"International Bicycle Touring Society. There are several biking societies in the U.S. The League of American Wheelmen, for instance, is a cracking good national lobbying group that's trying to get more bike trails authorized. To attain a fairer shake for cyclists in a world commanded by the horseless carriage. And there's the Bicycle Institute of America, which actively addresses itself to general promotion of the sport. Then there's the American Youth Hostels, which is great for your offspring but probably wouldn't be your cup of tea. And there's the IBTS. It grinds no axe. Its primary mission is to have fun. Naturally, that's the one we've been most active in."

"That sounds like my cup of tea."

"It was organized, oddly enough, by a California surgeon named Clifford Graves, who happens to have a passion for pedaling. People from all walks of life and every age group have joined in a sort of loosely knit society, dubbed the 'Huff and Puffers.' It's a completely nonprofit operation. Dr. Graves and his volunteer helpers listen to anyone who has a good idea for a cycling tour. Then they lay out a route, line up hotels along the way, charter a sag wagon, and pass the word. People show up from some of the damnedest places."

"I've managed to avoid guided tours like the plague. But this sounds like fun."

"It's a blast. Informal as hell, and you have all the advantages of group travel without the disadvantage of regimented riding. Members range from twenty-four to seventy-two. If you want to see a generation de-gapper, you should take a trip with this outfit."

"This French tour will be our seventh with the 'Huff and Puffers,' " said Jean. "We have a sag-wagon driver who takes our baggage on ahead and checks us into our next stop. We always have a delightful place to pull into for the night. It really makes an enjoyable trip."

"Any chance of getting an itinerary?"

"It's being firmed up now," said Hartley. "We'll get one to you."

"Great. Let's drink to our invasion of Europe."

"Good idea."

We did.

Thanks to the advent of jet propulsion, it's easy to forget how big the good ole U.S.A. really is. When you can walk into a perambulating hotel lobby like the jumbo jet at Los Angeles and emerge four hours later in New York City, one is prone to ignore the tremendous amount of real estate that speeds by below. In spending five days of hard driving to achieve the same objective—which we hadn't done for years—distances once again assume their true meaning. Even with breather stops in Colorado and Washington, D.C., to visit old friends, it was a hard trip. And in a new air-conditioned Buick. I couldn't help wondering how it was going to be crossing Europe on bicycles.

It was our design to spend a few days with our daughter, Ann, and her husband, Pete, in New York City to regroup and pack for our two-wheeled expedition. This we did, and after three days in Fun City we were itching to get going. The fourth morning we caught the limousine for John F. Kennedy Airport.

Next stop, Frankfurt, Germany.

There is a travel book written by Arthur Frommer. It's called *Europe on $5 & $10 a Day*. No news to eight zillion people who have traveled to Europe. With the possible exception of *Portnoy's Complaint*, it's doubtful the winds of controversy have ever swirled more around a single publication. We were to see this tome praised to the heavens, and damned to eternal purgatory. We saw it in the hands of young travelers being clutched more firmly than their traveler's checks; we witnessed its acceptance as passports by a harried Swiss customs official trying to work through a train of college kids; we saw it in the hands of sightseers, its torn-out pages replacing the time-honored tourist guide; we saw it flung into the canals of Venice by a frustrated tourist.

Oddly enough, the very qualities of this Gawker's Gideon that make it so appealing are the very virtues that see it condemned. For by listing the addresses of good, clean European accommodations reasonably priced, the lodgings and restaurants endorsed by Frommer were generally packed with Americans. Not all bad, but one has more in mind rubbing shoulders with the Danes in Denmark and the French in France than having to fly clear across the ocean just to be crushed by busloads of conventioners from Perth Amboy, New Jersey.

We wanted to travel through Europe as economically as possible—a decision dictated not only by my bank balance, but by our desire to see if our cycling, coupled with the economies of living in the backcountry, could produce a delightful new way to see Europe on a shoestring. To this end, we armed ourselves with *Europe on $5 & $10 a Day*, and found that its assets far outweighed its liabilities.

We had arrived in Europe at the tail end of the tourist season, or between the "peak season" and the "shoulder season," as the travel agencies label it. By invading Denmark near the end of August, we felt we could take advantage of still mild weather, yet see the departure of the glut of college kids and tourists who had to get back to work. As planned, not only did we escape most of the annual migration from across the Atlantic, but as the first of September rolled around we started enjoying the first dip in the seasonal tourist rates.

One fact gleaned from Frommer proved worth its weight in traveler's checks: the recommendation that all train travel in Europe be second class. He maintained the difference between first and second class was the payment of 50 percent more money, for which you received two more inches of padding on the train seat. Also, by going first cabin you usually rode alone; with other Americans, or with some stuffy upper-class European—and you missed all the action in second class.

This was demonstrated during our train trip from Frankfurt to Copenhagen. On the advice of recent continental travelers I had procured one Eurailpass prior to leaving the States. This ingenious travel idea provided in one single, wallet-size ticket unlimited first-class rail travel throughout all Europe (British Isles excepted), and cost $160 for one month. I bought it as a sort of substitute sag wagon, in case bicycle breakdown, sickness, or some other emergency required speedy transportation. It proved to be a fantastic bargain.

Since I had my Eurailpass, I bought another first-class ticket for Dortha, and second-class tickets for Scott and Holly, who opted to ride where the action was. As predicted, Dortha and I found ourselves in a clean, very comfortable compartment. It was also empty, as was the rest of the whole first-class car. Finally tiring of watching northern Germany fly by, the two of us went back to visit our offspring in the second-class accommodations.

They were having a blast. A United Nations mixture of nationalities filled the six-seat compartment. A German lad had produced a yard-long sausage and a loaf of pumpernickel, a Dane's knapsack had yielded a round of excellent cheese, a Spanish student from Madrid passed around a goat bladder filled with wine. All were enthusiastically yapping a mile a minute in a duke's mixture of languages. We were invited to join the party, and we did. Before the trip was over we had met half the people in the car, had bridged the language gap with snatches of forgotten phrases, pantomime, gesticulations, and sign language; we had a ball. All too soon we had traversed northern Germany, boarded the train ferry at Puttgarden, sailed across the Baltic Sea to Denmark, and pulled into Copenhagen.

Tired but cheerful after the all-night trip, we found, with the help of Frommer's book, a pension that could manage four. An hour later we were at the doorstep of Mrs. Meta Jensen in a very quiet and respectable section of Copenhagen. A delightful woman, Mrs. Jensen took us into her heart as well as her home, and for the munificent sum of ten dollars a day for the four of us—including breakfast—we were made very comfortable in two spotlessly clean, commodious rooms, complete with huge eiderdowns that beckon a lodger to crawl in and hibernate for the winter.

We did hibernate for a couple hours to knit the frayed

nerves of the oldsters, who were not used to staying up all night. Then we all took hot baths and prepared ourselves for our expedition to the bicycle shop.

Mr. O. Norit was very definitely a gentleman of the old school. He owned a quaint and efficient bicycle shop on Copenhagen's bustling Kongevej Street, spoke limited but patient English, and was, according to the wife, a doll. He also bore a striking resemblance to Thumbelina's grandfather. In response to our question, he slapped his cheeks and smiled. Yes, he certainly did stock ten-speed bicycles.

There were several brands from which to choose. A heavy German make, a sturdy but ponderous Danish make, and the French Peugeot. It was the last that brought cries of joy from Holly, the most knowledgeable of any of us in the lore of the ten-speed. I hefted it, it was light. I bounced it, nothing fell off. It was beautifully enameled, the fittings were chrome, it had a Simplex derailleur, a bicycle pump, a generator that sparked headlight and taillight, fenders, a bell, a luggage rack, and reflectors on the pedals. "Has everything but a rumble seat," I said, smiling at Mr. Norit.

He nodded somberly. "The seat should not rumble. This is a *smuk* bicycle, a beautiful bicycle. The best we have."

I patted the skinny bicycle seat. It had the sponginess of a tire iron. "This is the softest seat you have?"

He looked at the seat, then looked at the part of my anatomy that would be embracing the seat. He nodded, reached behind a counter and came up with a sponge-rubber slipcover. He slipped it over the seat. "Better?"

"Now you're talking." I patted it again. It now had the sponginess of a tire iron covered with a slice of foam rubber. I tried to smile through clenched teeth. "What is the best price you can give me on four of these?"

"Four of them! Four ten-speed bicycles?"

I ticked off the Anderson tribe one by one. "Four. We're going to cycle through Europe. We need one apiece."

"My-oh-my! Four bicycles." It is doubtful if Mr. Norit had sold four ten-speeds all year. Danes love cycles, but with the flat terrain around Copenhagen there is little demand for ten gears. To get a request for four ten-speeds was like a Ford dealer in rural Alabama getting an order for four Lincoln Continentals. Mr. Norit, obviously flustered, excused himself. He went into the tiny cubicle of his office for a moment, then emerged with an invoice upon which he had been scribbling. "One hundred American dollars apiece." He smiled disarmingly.

"A hundred bucks apiece!" I prepared to go into my apoplectic shock routine that I always enact when dealing with car salesmen. Just on the verge of flinging myself on the floor and kicking my heels, I received a we-don't-haggle-with-Thumbelina's-grandfather look from the distaff. Checking myself, I said limply, "That includes the foam rubber seat covers, of course."

"No," said Mr. Norit.

Thumbelina's grandfather had evidently gone to school with Ralph Williams. "I just thought perhaps when ordering a third of a dozen bicycles, one might get some sort of a volume discount."

"No," said Mr. Norit.

I love bargaining, but knowing I'd have to overcome not only Mr. Norit but the wife as well, I threw in the towel. An hour later we had run up quite a bill. In addition to the bikes, we needed two seatcovers for the old folks (the siblings looking at them in disgust) for $1.50 apiece; four odometers to check our mileage each day—$2.50 apiece; four pant clips— $.50; four bungee cords for securing baggage—$1.00; and panniers. I wished I had picked up four sets of Hartley Alley's panniers before we left the States, as the only thing available was a set of aluminized saddlebags with a spring attachment that secured to the rear wheel. They were light and waterproof, so we felt we could make do—$4.50 a pair. With four pairs of tennis shoes designed for cycling—$6.50 a pair; four bicycle locks—$2.00 apiece; four yellow nylon windbreakers—$12.50 each; and a real bargain: four lightweight collapsible suitcases at $4.00 apiece that fit perfectly on the luggage rack over the panniers, we were in business. Our total cash outlay for our two-wheeled transportation came to around $135 per person. Not too bad, considering that the price in the States would have been that much for the bicycles alone.

Dortha and Holly each selected a small-sized men's bike, partly on the advice of the shopkeeper, for the added strength the straight bar provided the frame. Strength and durability, they thought, would be needed for extensive bike touring, particularly over some of the back roads we would encounter. I was skeptical, figuring the wife would have problems enough getting used to the new bike—having so long abstained from the sport—without the additional hassle of coping with the bar. I was outvoted, however, and we ended up with two large men's bikes for Scott and me, and two smaller men's bikes for the women. Since the latter had to be ordered from the warehouse, Mr. Norit said all four would be ready at noon the next day—assembled, tuned, greased, and ready to go. Then he presented the total bill, a great smile crowding his rosy cheeks.

I looked it over. "I don't suppose you'd take a personal check on a Stateside bank? I'd rather not spend my traveler's checks if I can help it."

The shopkeeper allowed this would present many problems to him, but his bank across the street loved to deal with such problems. Perhaps they would cash a personal check. I had my reservations, as it's difficult to cash a check at a different bank in the States, let alone one in Copenhagen. Nevertheless, Dortha and I went over to Den Danske Landsmandsbank across the street to find out.

A tall, gorgeous blonde—who I wished was the manager but wasn't—ushered us to the desk of a cheery, elegant Dane who was.

"I am Oskar Fjellander," he said in flawless English, rising to meet us. We shook hands. "What may I do for you?"

At least we weren't going to have to hurdle the language barrier. Introductions completed, I reached for my wallet containing my credentials. "I doubt if you can help us, sir, but I was wondering if it would be possible to cash a personal check on my bank in the States."

"Why is it you Americans all have such nice teeth?" he answered.

Knowing the question wasn't addressed to me, I turned to the wife, who at the moment was exhibiting hers. "It's because of a cult in the United States," she said. "We all worship a witch doctor called an orthodontist. We practice nifty puberty rites by stuffing lots of wire into the mouths of children, and lots of greenbacks into the hands of the witch doctor."

"Marvelous," said the banker.

"You see, Mr. Fjellander," I ventured again, "we've made a substantial purchase at the bicycle shop across the street. Rather than exhaust my supply of traveler's checks, I was hoping—"

"Europeans have such bad teeth," he said. "Rotten. Even Crest doesn't help."

"But you have nice teeth," said the missus.

"Very nice of you to say that, Mrs. Anderson." He tapped them with his pencil. "Best porcelain money can buy."

I cleared my throat. "I have here a courtesy card from the Bank of America, a card of guaranteed credit from my banker, a—"

The manager looked down at the collection of celluloid that was littering his desk. "You certainly do have a nice collection of cards all right." He picked them up, then fanned them into a bridge hand. "But look at this hand. Looks like a foot."

"I'm sorry about that. If you want a new deck—"

"Do I understand correctly that you want to cash a personal check on your Stateside bank?"

"The thought did cross my mind, yes."

"Then please write out the check. Dispense with all this folderol." He handed back the cards. "What do you want? A thousand? Two thousand?"

"You mean just like that? You don't need my letter of cred——"

"Denmark is a very civilized country, my good man. Write out the check for whatever amount you need. I'll initial it, then just take it to the cashier." He turned to the wife. "Tell me, Mrs. Anderson, if I'm not being too personal. Do you use a Waterpik?"

Scandinavians are something else. Maybe it stems from the strain of some Nordic iceman that filtered into my genealogy in centuries gone by, but whatever it is, my romance with these handsome people has been going on for a long time. I'm sure their great sense of humor has a lot to do with it, as does their industriousness, their demand for cleanliness, their exuberant approach to life. And all this is reflected in their country, even including the big cities.

There are only several exceptions to my dislike of big cities and wonderful, wonderful Copenhagen happens to be one of them. More than five thousand years ago the first Stone Age hunters and fishermen hunkered down on what is now the main shopping street to wolf their raw fish and eels. And around 1040, Hafnia became the nucleus of a far-reaching trade for

merchants from the entire Baltic area, hence its name Koben-
havn or Copenhagen, meaning merchant's harbor. In 1167
Bishop Absalon built his stone fortress, the foundations of
which can be seen today in the cellars of Christiansborg Palace.
In the seventeenth century, King Christian IV, a hep old gent,
was the town's first great builder and is responsible for the
physical structure of what is considered today one of Europe's
most delightful and beautiful cities.

To the Danes' credit—unlike some cities such as Rome,
which has gone bankrupt trying to resolve the knuckle-biting
contrast between preserving history, yet preparing for the
future—the Danes have managed to amalgamate the two: main-
taining the flavor, artifacts, and history of the Old World, while
still making seven-league strides into the future—hand in hand
with indoor plumbing. Wide, flower-bedecked, spotlessly clean
avenues (have they developed some kind of dog food that self-
destructs?); handsomely preserved churches; the Royal The-
ater; the Town Hall; Amalienborg, the royal residence; the fascinating museums—all blend harmoniously with the most beautiful shops, office buildings, and up-to-date department stores in
the world.

That afternoon we toured the Paris of the North. After a
delicious "Danwich" meal—succulent open-faced sandwiches
lathered with marinated herring, smoked eel, liver paste, and
the pearllike minishrimp from local waters—the younger set
peeled off for a bus tour to see the city sights; the idea had
needed little encouragement once Scott discovered the tour terminated at the Carlsberg brewery, where visitors were permitted to partake freely of the excellent Danish beer. The frau
and I went window-shopping, strolling down Copenhagen's fantastic Stroget, drooling at the impressive Danish furniture, furs,
porcelain, glass, and silver in shopwindows.

We had tea at one of the sidewalk cafés and watched the
Copenhagen citizenry stroll by: longhairs with guitar in hand

mingling with well-dressed businessmen carrying briefcases; housewives pushing fancy prams; a sari-clad Indian from the local embassy walking with a handsomely bearded mariner who must have been a whaler captain from Greenland. And woven throughout this tapestry of personalities were the gorgeous young Danish women, their long, golden shanks flashing from high-fashion miniskirts.

At happy hour we rejoined the offspring at Tivoli Gardens. The enchanting Tivoli! Incongruously, these world-famous gardens that provide joy to many thousands daily were laid out a century and a half ago on parts of Copenhagen's old fortifications; and the small electric boats filled with happy people are humming around a lake that was at one time a heavily defended moat.

We strolled through its banks of flowers, taking the late afternoon sun with the Danes, who covered the spectrum of age: the tots joyously immersed in ice cream cones; the septuagenarians smoking cigars—the elegant dames lighting up their cheroots and their pipes right along with their men. And when night fell, the gardens took on a completely new look under the illumination of twinkling colored lamps in a breathtaking fairyland. We wandered among the dozen orchestras and bands, like kids on their first day at Disneyland, drinking in the delights.

We ate dinner at one of the outdoor restaurants, gorging on fresh Scandinavian seafood that we washed down with schooners of the incomparable Danish beer. Then we attended an excellent concert, chuckled over a pantomime comedy, and ate the weight watcher's nightmare known as Amerikaner ice cream cones. Finally knuckling under to a metabolic time clock that was chiming on Stateside time, we headed for the Tivoli gates just as the fireworks erupted in a booming phantasmagoria of crackling color.

A fitting end to a glorious day.

3

Shaken Up by the Shakedown Cruise

AT precisely noon the next day we were at Mr. O. Norit's bicycle shop. Inside, the four bikes were all lined up in a neat row, the paint gleaming, the chromium flinging back the sun of a brilliant day. They looked beautiful.

Mr. Norit came out of his little cubicle, beaming and dry-washing his hands. "*Ja*. The cycling Andersons. As you can see, your bicycles are ready."

As we each examined our new possessions, I noticed something had been added to mine. A small, elegant, antique brass horn with a rubber bulb had replaced the standard bell on the handlebars. Delighted, I gave the bulb a squeeze. A magnificent, raucous honk bellowed from the horn. I grinned at the shop owner. "This is beautiful, Mr. Norit. Where did you get it?"

He dismissed the question with a wave of his hands. "Just a little gift. For the—" he thumped his forehead with the heel of his hand, trying to surface the word. "You know. On your Gunsmuk television—the wagon keeper?"

"Wagon master."

He clapped his cheeks. "*Ja ja.* The wagon master. That is you." I thanked him profusely for the gift. He said: "Why not try your new bicycles?"

"Good idea. We'll take a little spin around the block." In a flash the youngsters had wheeled their bikes out the door, mounted them, and dissolved easily into the noontime traffic of the busy street. I assisted Dortha to the curb with hers and helped her straddle it.

Used to a lady's bike, the bar gave her a little trouble. It took some doing before she finally managed to get a leg over it. "You sure, Andy, our insurance is up to date? Our will is in order? And everything?"

"Just concentrate on the bicycle, dear." I noticed she was in an awkward position. When she reached down to grasp the brake levers on the handlebars, she appeared to be standing on her head. "Your seat should be lowered. And your handlebars raised."

"I'll try it around the block," she said nervously. "Then we can adjust it." She pushed off the curb. There was a squeal of brakes as a truck screeched to a stop behind the wobbling bicycle. This was scarcely a confidence-building maneuver. She came back to the curb, and in the process squeezed her brake levers too hard. A wide slice of daylight developed between rider and cycle. I caught her just before she capsized.

"You're doing fine, dear. Downtown Copenhagen is not the best place to try out a new bicycle. If you can just make it to the side street down there, you'll be out of the noontime rush."

"To the side street," she muttered through dry lips. Taking advantage of a lull in traffic I launched her again, then stepped into her lane to ward off oncoming vehicles. I handled the flow on her side of the street, but was not prepared for the cars coming the other way, which, to my horror, she was weaving into. A great trumpet of unfriendly horns drove her back into her own lane, and weaving a drunken course she finally made the turn into the side street. My heart momentarily quit hammering my rib cage.

I jumped on my machine and followed. I began to understand Dortha's problem. Instead of sitting erect in the saddle as on a conventional bike, a touring cycle provides an uncomfortable proximity between nose and kneecap. Picking up several horn toots of my own, not to mention several unprintable Danish words, I wheeled off onto the side street. Preparing to confront the ghastly carnage of my favorite wife spread-eagled under her ten-speed, I caught instead a glimpse of upended fanny just turning the far corner, rotating like a piston engine. It was obvious that once she got started, the redhead was not about to stop until she reached her destination. And she obviously couldn't wait to reach her destination.

Circling the block, I pulled up in front of the bicycle shop to confront two jubilant offspring and a panting wife who looked as if she had just swum the Hellespont. "Well, dear," I said, striking a false air of confidence, "great bikes, wot?"

From my mate I received a look generally reserved for heroin pushers and encyclopedia salesmen. "Am I going to have to bike through Europe standing on my head? I've got a stiff neck trying to see where I'm going. And I only went around one block."

"I think your seat altitude needs adjusting."

"Not to mention my mental attitude."

Mr. Norit appeared upon the scene. He appraised the ungainly position of my inverted roommate. "We seem to have a problem," he said, giving voice to the understatement of the year.

Assisting Dortha off her bike, he produced a wrench and tackled the ten-speed. For some reason the seat had been raised several inches from the frame. He lowered it. Then he moved to the front and brought the handlebars up a couple inches. He cinched the bolts down tight, then asked the distaff to remount.

She did—this time assuming a more comfortable position on the machine. She could even see ahead of her without undue craning of the neck, and her posterior assumed a much more ladylike attitude. "Now, that's more like it," she said, looking pleased. "The blood isn't even rushing to my head."

"Most people," said Mr. Norit, "find a touring bike not comfortable at first. Later on you find travel easier and more comfortable over long distances with your body in a—" he substituted known gesticulations for unknown words.

"Horizontal position," I said, helping out.

"*Ja. Tak.*"

"I'm afraid," said Dortha, "I'm going to find my body in a horizontal position sans bicycle."

Norit spanked his cheeks at the thought. "Oh, no. I bet you want to lower the handlebars later on. To reduce—" he blew through puffed cheeks.

"Wind resistance," I added.

"*Ja.* Wind resistance."

I was happy to see the color returning to Dortha's face as she grinned. "Wind resistance, Mr. Norit, is not one of my problems at the moment. Try survival."

"You're a plucky little lass," I said, patting her shoulder.

"Ha. It's my plucky little lass I'm worried about."

I turned my attention to Scott and Holly. Having had no trouble at all mastering their equipment, they were full of vociferous adulation for the light, swift machines. They were also chafing to get going. "Mr. Norit," I said, "before we head south, I think it prudent we take a short shakedown cruise. Then you can make adjustments or solve any problems before we start our long journey."

He nodded in agreement. "*Ja. Det er godt.* Where do you plan to go?"

"Thought we might cycle north, up to Helsingör. Take the ferry from there to Sweden. Then bike down the Swedish coast a way, and return to Copenhagen on the ferry at Landskrona. How does that sound?"

"*Udmaerket!* And when you get back, bring in the bicycles. I will go over them *godt* before you go on your long trip."

Searching out quiet side streets, we managed to get the bikes to Mrs. Jensen's house without further incident. Then finding a suitable cul-de-sac nearby, Holly spent part of the afternoon working with the three of us, checking us out in the proper care, feeding, and riding of the ten-speed. Dortha was doing much better since her body was not in a downhill position all the time, and slowly she began to polish her rusty prowess with the two-wheeler. By the time night fell and forced us to suspend practice, she was getting so she could kick off with barely a wobble.

That night we exchanged our two wheels for a four-wheeled taxicab and dined at Den Gyldne Fortun, a highly recommended restaurant near the Stroget. The historic old basement grill-bar dated back four hundred years and more than lived up to its reputation. Our meals came to less than three dollars apiece, and were excellent. We spent a charming evening in the romantic candlelit atmosphere, supping with the ghosts of King Christian IV and Hans Christian Andersen —former frequenters of the establishment.

Then home to pack for our first trip on the morrow. We found that most of our luggage fit into the bike carriers and suitcases. The exceptions: Scott's *Playboy*s; Holly's gallon jug of hair shampoo; two of Big Red's girdles ("I'll lose so much weight I surely won't need these"); and a bottle of Scotch. These, along with two empty suitcases, were willed to Mrs. Jensen. A very fitting farewell gift to a proper, prim, teetotaling, Danish grandmother.

And then to the sack, slavering in joyous anticipation of the morning and our first day on the bikes.

All packed and ready to go, I assembled the troops for a last-minute briefing at the curb in front of the Jensen house. "All right, men, we're facing a tough foe. We're hitting the Copenhagen traffic at its worst—the morning rush hour. We're going to travel in single file, and stay close together going through the city. When I give three blasts on my horn like this"—I squeezed the bulb three times, sending the Jensen cat scurrying up the nearest tree—"that means pull over and stop. If we get strung out and anyone has a problem, jangle your bike bell three times. When you hear the bell, relay it along the line.

"I'll lead, since I have the map. Scott, you bring up the rear. Ride interference behind Ma. We're gonna take it easy at first, 'til we break in rusty muscles. Later on we can spread out a bit, each hitting his own stride. Okay. Any questions?"

"Just one," said Dortha. "How do you transfer out of this CS outfit?"

"No transfers until this mission is accomplished. Everybody set?" Two heads nodded, one shook. "All right, men. *Mount up!*" I gave a blast on the horn, and off we went.

There were a few harrowing moments when we wove into the thick work-bound traffic on our way out of the city. Although Dortha was demonstrating good progress in her mastery of the spoked wheel, her self-confidence was not keeping pace. She did fine riding along with the street to herself, but when she had to share it with other vehicles she was easily intimidated by the toot of a car. And a blast from a truck air horn really set her front wheel wobbling.

She was not alone. In this early stage none of us had learned to ride relaxed. Little wonder the Europeans, used to seeing Americans riding by in their big cars and touring buses, craned their necks at this column of yellow-jacketed cyclists hunched over their machines—each with fanny high, head low, white-knuckle grip on the handlebars, lips pressed into a death-defying grimace as they pedaled through the early morning traffic.

More than one startled traffic cop gave us the right-of-way through the traffic as if we were some courtly processional from the palace; drivers scraped fenders gawking at us; pedestrians stopped in their tracks thinking they were witnessing the last leg of a six-day bike race. Although cyclists were legion in the city, the ten-speed was still very much a rarity, and at every stop sign we would be surrounded by riders staring in open-mouthed wonder at this herd of strange-geared beasts.

We followed a route marked out on a cycling map Norit had given me. To our occasional consternation we found the cycling paths that separated us from traffic in the downtown district had a nasty habit of petering out at the most implausible places. Like a busy intersection. Leaving us at the mercy of congestion at its thickest. As we neared the outskirts of the city, however, the traffic thinned, good bicycle paths became the rule, and we all began to breathe more easily.

We finally reached Langelinie, and rode up it to where the famous Little Mermaid looks wistfully out over the sea. Here we pulled up for a well-deserved rest. We dismounted, congratulating one another for successfully spawning upstream through the worst traffic Copenhagen had to offer; and gawked at the pretty bronze sculpture of Hans Christian Andersen's most popular fairy-tale character.

In spite of losing her head recently to a despicable act of

vandalism, the mermaid had been restored to her pristine beauty, thanks to the preservation of the original mold which enabled her head to be recast on her body.

Refreshed and in a mood of jubilation, we remounted and pressed on northward up the beach road toward Helsingör. We rolled along the flat, windless cycle path, and in spite of threatening skies the cycling was exhilarating. Dortha waxed ecstatic over the magnificent suburbs of northern Copenhagen, where handsome pillared homes looked out over the sea, wearing lap robes of rolling green lawn that had never known the ulterior designs of dandelions or crabgrass. The path rolled right along the beach, and to the right we could see Sweden across the water, a touch of gray lumping the horizon.

Coming to a wide cycling road I dropped back to ride abreast of the redhead. The kids had gone on ahead, cruising at their own speed. "You know, honey," she said, surprising herself as much as me, "this is downright enjoyable. The scenery is breathtaking!"

"This is the Danish Riviera. It's beautiful."

"Look over there." She nodded to the left. "Looks like a little forest."

"According to my map, that's Klampenborg Deer Park. Herds of red and fallow deer roam there. That building up ahead should be the royal hunting lodge. It's still used."

"It's out of this world. No wonder people like to come to Denmark."

"You can't say the Danes discourage visitors. They probably have the sharpest tourist bureau in the world. They've laid on vacations now where you can stay at farms and live right with the farmers. Or rent a log cabin in the mountain ranges, if that's your bag. Or you can vacation in fishermen's dwellings in the Lofoten Isles. These Danes don't miss a trick."

"Well, devious or not, they certainly get my vote. I love them."

Up ahead I noticed the cycling path petering out, to make a short detour onto the beach road. "You go on ahead, honey," I said. "Short detour coming up, I'll drop back into single file."

"You just want to get in back and watch my bottom bounce."

"You guessed it. Really turns me on." I dropped back, allowing her to proceed ahead onto the narrow shoulder.

And then it happened!

Dortha dutifully swung out onto the road. She no sooner had done so than a car came from behind at a lively clip. It honked its horn in warning. Frightened by the klaxon she swung to the right to allow plenty of passing room. She was not prepared for the tall curb that suddenly materialized in front of her. She smashed into it.

Horrified, I watched her tumble over the handlebars. She flew through the air to land on her head and shoulders in a sickening motion. She did a complete somersault before coming to rest in a heap under her bicycle. It was a very nasty spill.

I leaped from my bike while it was still traveling, and dashed to her side. I bent over her, hesitating to touch her for fear of broken bones, and too shocked to do anything but stare at the crumpled heap of my beloved. Then she stirred. "Easy, honey," I said. "Is there anything broken?"

I picked the bike off her as she slowly rose to a sitting position. She shook her head, passing a palm over her eyes. "Oh, my God!" Then she looked at me, her eyes coming slowly into focus. "Wha' hoppen?"

"I'm not sure. But you really took a header. You sure you haven't broken anything?"

"My bike!" She looked around frantically. "I haven't broken my bike?"

"That's the least of our worries. Have you broken your body?"

She gingerly passed her hands over her torso. "No. I don't think so. Most of the parts seem to be here."

The car that honked at Dortha came backing up the road. The driver, a well-dressed Danish gentleman, hastily climbed out and rushed over to us. He spoke no English, but it was obvious he was shaken and very apologetic. Through sign language and painful smiles Dortha finally convinced him she was not hurt, and she didn't need to be taken to the nearest hospital. I wasn't nearly so sure, but taking my cue from the redhead we dismissed him with our thanks. Reluctantly he drove off, still apologizing.

With great care I helped Dortha to her feet, lest we cause other cars to notice the cyclist lying at the side of the road and stop. I felt her over carefully, dusting the dirt from her clothes. "Will you kindly watch your hands?" she said. "Ouch!"

"Aha! You are hurt."

"Just my dignity and my pride. And maybe the left knee is a little sore."

I pulled up her torn pants leg. The skin had been scraped on her knee, and it appeared swollen. "I think we'd better hail down a car. You shouldn't be walking on that leg, let alone riding."

"Nonsense." She looked down at her scuffed and smudged pantsuit. "It's just that I feel so foolish! I've got all the coordination of a spastic puppy. Let's check the bike."

"Will you quit worrying about the bike? Bikes are expendable. Wives aint. Walk a little bit. Over to that tree and back."

She protestingly obliged, limping a little. "See? I'm all right. Now can we check the bicycle?"

"In a minute." I drew her to me and pulled out my handkerchief. "Spit."

"Oh, for heaven's sake—"

"*Spit!*" She made a wry face and moistened my handkerchief. I wiped the grime off her face. In the process I uncovered a big bump on her forehead. Also a marked swelling around the right eye. "Know what, love?"

"Yes, I know what. I know now why kids hate to have their face washed with their own spit."

"You, my dove, are going to have a shiner. One big, beautiful mouse."

"Oh, no!"

"Afraid so. Furthermore, we're going to have a doctor look at you. You could have gotten a concussion from that fall."

"Poppycock!" She turned from me and went to her bicycle. "I'm fine. Now will you *please* check my bike? We've got a lot of miles to make." She pointed down the road to where the kids had stopped and were looking back curiously. She grinned and waved. They motioned impatiently.

I checked the bicycle. To my surprise, except for several scratches on the chromium and an askew handlebar, there appeared to be no damage. My estimation of the Peugeot went up sharply. Gripping the front wheel between my legs, I pulled the handlebars back straight.

"Thank you." She straddled her obstreperous steed and started down the road. I watched her for a moment and saw that her wheels were tracking true. I sighed, and got back on my machine.

We had survived the first calamity.

I hoped.

Lunchtime found us at Skodsborg, an enchanting little fishing village right on the sound. The Skodsborg Kro, a popular seafood restaurant, had been recommended to us, and we had no trouble finding the picturesque café. We were shown an outside table on a terrace overlooking the sea. Our beginning-to-complain muscles were soon forgotten as we drank in the flavor of the quiescent spot. Fishing boats were mirrored in the calm sea, and only the lament of wheeling gulls punctuated the stillness.

While waiting to order, Dortha excused herself to repair her damaged makeup. I talked the waiter out of some ice and wrapped it in a napkin. When she returned I made her lean back in her chair, and applied the cold pack to her head. Her protestations diminished to a murmur as the cold seeped into her feverish brow. I noticed, without commenting, that her right eye was considerably swollen. "We're not going to try and make Helsingör tonight," I said. "After lunch we're pulling into the first decent hotel. I'm going to have that eye looked at."

"Will you quit babying me?" Her good eye spat sparks from under the napkin. "No reason at all why we can't make our objective."

"My love." I patted her hand. "I don't like the looks of that eye." I glanced up at an ominous black cloud building up in the north. "And I don't like the looks of that thunderhead. It's going to rain. Now am I not the wagon master?"

"You are the wagon master," chorused the crew, batoned by Holly's fork. "You are the wagon master."

"Then so be it."

Refueled with a round of frosty-glassed Tuborg beer and an excellent lunch of open-faced sandwiches, the morale of the group rose considerably. Only one incident marred the lunch hour—when Holly elected to investigate a pet monkey that was caged in an enclosure on the terrace. Bending close to talk to it, she discovered the monkey was not too enthused about dialogue, but was very interested in the gold-framed glasses she was wearing. Before she realized what was happening, a small paw snaked out through the cage, and presto! The monkey was wearing them.

Not really believing what I was seeing, I dispatched Scott to find the manager, while we all breathlessly watched the simian doing unspeakable things with Holly's glasses—the pair that had been specially ordered for bike riding. The incident soon became a production.

No one on the premises could find the key to the monkey cage. This required dispatching a runner to track down the animal's keeper, who lived next door. While all this was going on, Holly was talking to the pet, intoning about the drastic consequences of wearing someone else's prescription. The simian, busily engrossed in staring at objects made fascinating by the distorting lenses, had no intention of giving them back. Instead, he jumped up and down and raced around the pen like a bespectacled Peter Pan.

Finally tiring of wearing them, the monkey had just decided to eat them when the keeper arrived on the scene. He didn't have a key either. It was fortunate, therefore, that he did have a way with primates. Bribing it with a banana, the keeper managed to reach the culprit and interest him in his offering. The apeling considered it for a moment, none of us daring to breathe, as he weighed the pros and cons of appetite versus curiosity. Then he reached for the banana. At the same time dropping the glasses. The keeper made a lunge and caught them just before they'd have smashed on the brick floor of the cage.

The breath locked in four chests exploded simultaneously. I took the glasses from the keeper, replacing them with a crisp bill. The man flashed a toothless grin of thanks between apologies to us and rebukes at the simian. Since he was speaking Danish the words meant no more to us than they did to the primate, but the understanding was there. He bowed to us, then firing one more volley of reprimand at the unreprimandable monkey, he hightailed it back to finish his lunch.

"Well," said Holly, as we prepared to mount up and depart, "I never dreamed bicycling could be so much fun."

"A laugh a minute," I said.

"Come to think of it, it's a good thing I wasn't wearing my contacts." She looked at me through spectacles now bearing the faint marks of monkey teeth. "If that monkey takes a shine to contacts—zap! Just like that, out could come an eyeball."

I looked at my cute daughter and shuddered. "That's a horrible thought. After your mom's accident we only have seven good eyes between us as it is. Please stay away from monkey cages."

"Aye aye, skipper."

Around midafternoon, according to our odometers and my leg muscles, we had covered twenty-five miles. Plenty, I figured, for our first day, especially considering we'd spent nearly an hour in the traffic of Copenhagen. I had wanted to stop at several inviting inns along the way in view of the wife's condition, but she turned deaf ears.

She *had* acquiesced to drop into the nice little hotel when we reached Humlebæk, for a cup of tea, and to allow Scott to prowl through the nearby Louisiana Art Gallery. This he wanted to do because it contained a fine collection of modern Danish and international art and was reputed to be one of the finest galleries in Europe. With the troops off ogling Rembrandt and Van Gogh, I looked my wife squarely in her puffy eye. "Honey, this is a nice little inn. Let's cave in right here for the night. Doctor that eye."

She shook her head. "I refuse to be an anchor on this tour. Besides, I think it would be fun to make it to Helsingör. I'd like to spend the night with Hamlet's ghost at Kronborg Castle."

"I have it from a reliable source he's not seeing visitors. Not only that, but he's got a thing about redheads." I looked out the window. "Besides, those storm clouds are beginning to produce. I noticed several drops—"

"You a fair-weather bike rider?"

"I know enough to come in out of the rain."

"You said Helsingör was only six or seven miles up the road from here. We can do it easily. Now quit arguing."

I sighed. "I should kick your backside."

She grimaced. "Oh. Please don't. It's sore enough already."

We had gone several miles since leaving the inn. The rain was coming down in a fine drizzle, and the bicycle path had turned into a sidewalk, forcing us to cycle along the shoulder of the road. The youngsters, as usual, were far ahead. Dortha brought up the rear so she could set her own pace. A car came speeding up from the rear and released a warning bellow from its horn.

And then it happened again.

This time I didn't see the accident. I heard it. Shortly after the sound of the horn there was a high-pitched oath, followed by the sound of scraping metal. And then an audible thump.

"Oh, good God!" I moaned, wheeling around. When I skidded up, Dortha was sitting in a large puddle in the middle of the sidewalk.

"Those damned curbs! Those miserable damned curbs!" She looked up at me through her one good eye, little rivulets of rain mixing with tears on her cheeks.

I sat down in the puddle with her and took her in my arms. "Sweetheart! Is anything broken?"

She buried her head in my chest. "Andy! I can't do it! I just can't do it. I'm making such an awful fool of myself. And I'm ruining the trip for you all!" She grabbed me tight, shaking and sobbing.

"It's all right. It's all right."

"Oh, honey! Why couldn't I be more coordinated? You hate me, don't you?"

"I love you. It's just that you got this thing about curbs."

"I'm such a clumsy, no-good, no-talent oaf. I could kill myself for being such an ass."

"I do wish you'd quit trying."

She looked up at me. "I'll bet you want a divorce. And I don't blame you one bit."

"I want you to quit talking gibberish. You didn't land on your head again?"

"No." She painfully rubbed her posterior. "I certainly did not."

"Look. The car's backing up. Now I'm going to have them take you to the nearest hotel. And no argument. See if you can get on your feet." I helped her up. "At least you didn't get all skinned up this time. Rain made the sidewalk slippery. Always something to be thankful for."

"If I've got so much to be thankful for, how come I look like the wreck of the Hesperus?"

I cupped her chin and pulled her face to mine. I started sponging off the mud with my wet handkerchief. The car pulled up and stopped. An elderly gentleman with a long, flowing moustache jumped out and ran over to us, spouting Danish a mile a minute. I stopped him with a raised palm. "Sorry. We're American. Don't speak Danish."

"Good. I don't speak it very well myself. I'm English. Reginald Spencer at your service." He turned to Dortha. "I saw you fall in the rearview mirror. Dreadfully sorry. Anything I can do?"

"You can pass a law outlawing the automobile horn," she said, trying to muster what dignity she could while wringing out a pantleg.

"My wife has a thing about getting honked at," I explained. "Seems to drive her into curbs."

"I'm terribly sorry. I wasn't honking *at* you, you know.

It's customary on a busy road in Denmark to honk so cyclists will know you're coming. It's a safety measure. After all, you cyclists have the right-of-way."

"I've been trying to remember that," said the redhead, "every time I take a half gainer into a cement sidewalk."

"Nasty business," said Spencer, sympathetically. "Allow me to make amends. Can I give you a lift?"

"You can," I said. "To the nearest hotel. We've had it for the day."

"There's a nice little inn up the road a few kilos. The Skotterup Kro in Espergærde. I'd be most happy to drive you there."

"But what about our bikes?" asked Dortha.

"I'll bring them," I said. "You go with Mr. Spencer. I'll meet you there."

"But—"

I looked sternly at my wife. "No buts. You get what's left of that little carcass of yours into Mr. Spencer's car. And as soon as I get to the hotel we'll find a doctor."

She started to argue, then saw the look in my eye. "Yes, dear."

I took her by the elbow and helped her into the front seat. I was closing the door when something coming up the road caught her eye. "Look!" she said. I looked. She was staring at a white-haired old lady tooting toward us on an ancient, dilapidated bicycle. Completely oblivious to the rain, the traffic, or the string of cars lined up patiently behind her, the octogenarian churned ahead, a stream of smoke trailing from an old corncob pipe clenched in toothless jaws. Coming abreast of the car parked on her side of the road, she gave several no-nonsense jangles on her bicycle bell to clear the way. As Spencer hugged the side of the car to make room, she sailed serenely by, like the Queen Mary putting out to sea.

"You see what I mean?" said Spencer. "Cyclists *do* have the right-of-way."

"That does it!" growled Dortha. She bolted from the car, limped over to her bicycle, and snatched it up. "That really rips it!" Before I realized what was happening, she had straddled her bike and was pedaling painfully down the road.

"*Hey!*" I yelled. "You come back here. Damn it, woman, *come back!*"

"Meet you at the hotel in Espergærde," she threw back over her shoulder.

I watched her, hunkered down into the rain, pedaling gamely. I could see her rear fender was askew, rubbing the tire. She, too, noticed it, and without even turning she reached back with her foot and gave it a swift kick. This miraculously knocked the fender back into alignment, and barely missing a stroke, she plunged on down the road.

"I say," said the Englishman, watching the retreating figure. "Did you see that? Bloody good show."

"There's going to be a bloody good show when I get her in that hotel room!"

"That's what I like in my women. Spirit! Fortitude!"

"If that's what you like in your women," I said, picking up my bicycle, "you'd go bananas over that one."

4

Different Spokes
for Different Folks

THE sun was poking sneaky fingers through the shutters of the
Skotterup Kro when I awoke the next morning. I stretched my
torso luxuriously under the thick comforters and immediately
regretted it. A muscle spasm shot along my leg and froze my
foot at a forty-five degree angle. I hopped out of bed cursing,
sending other muscles to twanging in sympathy. From hair root
to toenail I was one throbbing, protesting muscle.

"Why are you jumping around," asked the wife, peeking
out from under her comforter, "like a whooping crane in
heat?"

"Cramps!" I murmured through clenched teeth, kneading
my calf.

"I didn't know men got the cramps."

"Very funny. Quit making with the bad jokes and rub
my calf. My muscle's all tied up in a granny knot."

Dutifully she sat up, pulled my leg into her lap and started
massaging it. "You *sure* this is in our marriage contract?"

54

"Positive. Don't talk. Rub." Slowly my frozen leg began to thaw. "I seem to be a bit stiff this morning."

"I wonder why. Just once maybe you'll get into condition before you tackle one of your outings. You know, sort of tune up."

"I'm in great shape, woman. Joe Namath has muscle spasms."

"Joe Namath has muscles."

I looked over at my wife. A testy retort died on my lips. "Good grief, honey! You don't look like you feel very good."

She touched her swollen eye. "I certainly don't feel like I look very good." And she didn't. Her right eye was a slit in a technicolored goose egg, and her forehead wore a large, bruised bump. She covered her face with her hands. "If you think this end looks bad, you should see the other end. Man has invented no more heinous tool of torture than a touring-bicycle seat. My derriere looks like a Toulouse-Lautrec painting."

"Let me see it."

She slapped my hands. "Not on your life, Dirty Old Man. Some things are sacred."

"Then that settles it. We're going nowhere today. We're going to stay in our lair and lick our wounds."

"That's exactly what we're *not* going to do. We're going to get on our bikes and ride the stiffness out of our sore muscles."

"Oh ho! Now lookee here—"

"Now *you* lookee here. The doctor told us last night there was nothing wrong with me. Just a few bruises and scratches, and they'll go away. We're going to rout the kids out of bed, eat a good breakfast, and be on our way."

I chucked her under the chin. "Am I to gather from this conversation you're not in the mood to curl up under these warm covers and fool around a little?"

"*Fool around a little!* As sore as I am? You so much as touch me and I'll scream my head off!"

"I'll go pack the bicycles."

A high-pressure area had sent the storm clouds packing, and it was a beautiful morning as we wheeled the bikes out of the shed and prepared to mount up. I went in to settle our bill, curious as to how much a night in a small Scandinavian hotel would cost.

We had been warned that Denmark is one of the most expensive European countries, partly because of a recently levied tax called "moms" (pronounced "mumps" for obvious reasons). Levied in 1970, this tax added 15 percent to the price of goods and services. This, in addition to the usual 15 percent service charge, adds a whopping 30 percent to the bills of all hotels and restaurants. A nifty device for letting visiting firemen help subsidize Denmark's government—proving the Danes don't take too many stupid pills. Private homes, happily, are exempt from these surcharges, and it was in these dwellings we hoped to stay most of the time.

Settling the bill, I was pleasantly surprised. Our full-course dinner (chicken cooked in creamed shrimp sauce that sounds awful but tastes delicious) was less than $3.00 apiece, including beverages. And our night's stay in the charming seaside hotel—with balconied rooms overlooking the sound—came to $5.50 per person, "moms" and breakfast included. The continental breakfast consisted of a soft-boiled egg, half a dozen different types of bread and rolls, excellent Danish butter, jams, and coffee. And as an added bonus, our bathless rooms afforded an excellent opportunity to meet people from all nations as we gathered in line for the one john that serviced each floor. All in all, a thoroughly delightful experience.

We were glad it was just a short ride to Helsingör. Although leg muscles began to lose their soreness after several miles, each of us found his respective coccyx did not, and the thin foam rubber on our bicycle seats had turned into very thick cockleburs. I sat up on my seat, back on my seat, side-saddle on my seat. There was just no way to comfortably adjust 190 pounds of beef on a six-inch pivot without exerting tremendous pressures on each tender square inch.

And Dortha, bravely plugging along beside me on a wide cycle path, was not without her problems. Not that she looked too bad—a scarf covered the knot on her head, wraparound sunglasses covered her shiner, and pancake makeup pretty well covered the rest—but her poop deck also refused to cooperate. I noticed her standing up on her pedals whenever she got the chance.

"I think we'd better get some talcum powder, honey," I said. "Help lubricate the squeaky joints."

She looked at me, trying to smile. "This is ridiculous. Trying to fit a size twelve fanny on a size two seat. I've got an acute case of cactus crotch."

"Only takes a little conditioning, dear. You'll be surprised how fast those tender parts will toughen. You'll be able to bust broncos in no time. Bareback."

"I think I've already busted something. Aint no bronco."

"That's Helsingör right up ahead. While the kids scout the castle, you and I'll find a nice park bench and snooze in the sun."

"Now you're talking my language."

Helsingör is a bright, friendly city. We pointed out the direction of the castle to the young ones, and since we'd seen it on a previous visit, sent them on their way to tour the magnificent, thousand-year-old moated fortress that was Shakespeare's setting for *Hamlet*. While the progeny stalked the ramparts looking for Hamlet's ghost, Big Red and I located a park bench overlooking the sound. We leaned our bikes against the seawall and did, indeed, snooze in the warm sun.

The troops returned, Scott bubbling with enthusiasm about the castle's possibilities for artistic renderings; Holly complaining about Hamlet being a Dirty Old Ghost who she swore materialized while she was in the castle's ladies' room. We discussed all this at length while biking the short distance to the ferry terminal where we were to embark for Sweden.

I hurdled the language barrier at the ticket office with a pantomime act that would have sent Marcel Marceau tripping to the showers. Although it was customary for cyclists to take their bicycles on one of the large car ferries, I found we could take our bikes on the passenger ferry.

As we were sitting in the passenger lounge an untoward thing happened. Probably not since the inception of the ferry service had one of the boats opted to drive right into the waiting room. For reasons best known to practitioners of the maritime profession, something went awry with the usually smooth-flowing channel traffic. Instead of gently nudging alongside the passenger pier, the boat picked this particular time to enter head-on. There was a hellacious crash and one side of the waiting room dissolved in a mass of splinters and flying glass.

Fortunately, the only serious injury was to the skipper's ego, and dusting off glass and splinters we took the side of discretion over valor, turned in our passenger boat tickets, picked up our bikes, and made a coward's retreat to the big-mawed car ferry that was loading nearby.

"What is there about us," asked Dortha, as we wheeled our bikes into the bowels of the big ship, "that seems to court catastrophe? Passenger ferries don't crash into waiting rooms. I'll bet that's the first time that ever happened."

"We're where it's at, Ma," said Holly, tying her bike to the ship in the section reserved for bicycles. "We're where the action is."

"I hope this is not the way the whole trip is going to be. I'm for a little less action and a little more relaxin'."

"I'm with you, Ma," I said, snugging up the bikes. "From now on it'll be smooth sailing." I looked up just in time to yank her out of the path of a long string of freight cars that was rumbling into the hold.

She caught her breath, then looked up at me out of her good eye. "You wanna bet?"

It was a very pleasant fifteen-minute journey across the narrow sound from Denmark to Sweden. We had a cup of coffee in the lounge of the huge, modern ferryboat and watched the long line of Scandinavians queueing up to purchase tax-free items on the high seas. Entirely too soon we pulled into the berth at Hälsingborg, Sweden.

Sweden! Land of the midnight sun, tall men, buxom women, warmth, humor, and hospitality. The country that leads the world in antipoverty, slum clearance, elegant suburbia, experimental marriage, and social security from the womb to the tomb. The price tag for all this also makes it the world leader in the high cost of living.

As we pedaled through the downtown district of Hälsingborg, it was difficult to reconcile this gracious, old-world town with progressive Sweden. The "Pearl of the Sound" is a sublime fairy-tale city stemming from the tenth century, when someone thought its high hill would make an excellent vantage point and forthwith planted a fortress on top.

We wove through its noontime traffic, accompanied by the first-blush thrill of entering a new country: senses suffused by the sight and smell of different customs and cultures. Dortha and Holly, finding window-shopping difficult to do from the curb, dismounted and walked their bikes along the intriguing shopwindows. Scott screeched to a halt to ogle the unabashed pornography displayed in a magazine kiosk. I, as usual, buried myself in my map trying to locate the least populated road out of town.

The course finally charted, I heeded a nudge from nature and went in search of the nearest men's room. The town's main street terminated abruptly at the base of the cliff overhanging the city. Steep steps rose from the street to wend heavenward up the tall hill to the castle on top. It was under these steps at street level I found a door that could lead only to a W.C. There was a uniformed man in evidence, further confirming my conclusion. "Is this the men's room?" I asked the attendant, trying not to cross my legs.

The uniformed man nodded grandly and held out his hand. I put a coin in it. He beckoned me into the inner chamber. I went in, followed by the attendant. He shut the door. I looked around for the porcelain furnishings that generally decorate the room I had in mind. There were none. I looked questioningly at the Swede. He smiled back, then pushed a button. The room mysteriously began to rise.

To my discomfort, I divined we were going somewhere in an elevator. Attempts at verbal communication were met only with a warm smile. I smiled back through gritting teeth, sincerely hoping that wherever we ended up there would be flushing furniture.

Several minutes later the door in the back of the elevator opened. The operator dismissed me, and I stepped out. I was on top of the cliff, at the foot of Karnan Castle. The view in every direction was spectacular. I thanked the elevator man. He smiled and went back into his yo-yoing chamber. Not pausing too long to savor the view, I spotted a little outdoor café to my right. With any luck at all, it would have a men's room.

It did. It was I who did all the smiling in the elevator on the way down.

Gathering up the troops, I broke the good news. "Have I found a great place for lunch! Lock your bikes and follow me."

"A nice little cozy tearoom?" asked the wife.

"A nice little tavern?" asked Scott.

"A boy's gym?" asked Holly.

"Better than that. And a view you won't believe." I ushered them toward the smiling attendant at the foot of the cliff. "We're going to eat in the men's room."

"How nice," said Dortha. "The men's room. That *will* be a view I won't believe."

We homesteaded a table on the outdoor terrace and sat down. For a moment we just drank in the view. The city below was a Disneyland set, the sea just beyond a speculum freckled with fishing boats and ferries plowing the narrow strait. It was a sight to behold.

Finally breaking the spell, I took orders for our lunch which had to be picked up at the self-service café.

"Just something to drink," said Holly.

"Like maybe a beer," said Scott.

I looked at them in surprise. "You've got to eat. That infernal cycling machine takes a lot of fuel."

"We have our lunch," said Holly. She opened her purse, a gunnysack affair she strapped to her bike, and started producing a stack of sandwiches wrapped in paper napkins.

"Where did you get those?" I asked.

"A little dividend from breakfast," said Scott. "We made sandwiches out of the stuff left over."

"You're kidding! Why, that's terrible!"

"While you ponder the impropriety of the act, Father," said Scott, "I'll go get us something to drink with them. One six-pack enough?"

As Scott departed, I looked over at the wife. "Do you see what these kids have done?"

"I do," said Big Red. "Aren't they great? Next time, Holly, make mine marmalade instead of jam."

"You!" I addressed the distaff. "The personification of

propriety. The instigator of integrity. Encouraging this sort of thing! Swiping food from a dining ro——"

"You're not looking at this thing in the proper perspective, Pop," said Holly. "The food was brought to the table for our consumption. Right? So what difference does it make if we eat it all for breakfast, or save some for lunch?"

"That's not the point. It's just not—"

"And who," chimed in Dortha, "always orders a doggy bag at a restaurant in the States? You're the only person in the world who takes home mashed potatoes."

"But—"

"This day and age," said Holly, "it is downright immoral to waste food. With millions of people suffering from malnutrition all over the world, it's a terrible crime to let anything go to waste."

"So there, wagon master," said the wife, grinning at me. "Anything else you'd like to say on the matter?"

"Yes," I said, biting into a thick sandwich. "Tomorrow, Holly, will you lay on a little more of that delicious Scandinavian butter?"

After lunch we skimmed along an excellent back road that unfolded its smooth surface along the coastline, sweeping by bustling marinas, fishing ports, and gorgeous vistas of the sound. The sun was shining, the weather downright balmy as we stripped our clothes down to the lowest layer permitted by decency. Although it was the last day of August, we were pleasantly surprised to find the climate of Scandinavia far milder than we had expected in these northern latitudes. In fact, more solar than polar, due to the gentle caresses of the Gulf Stream and the long sunlit nights of the summer season—a combination that provides excellent biking weather from April through October.

Sailing along in a mood of elation on the quiet, trafficless road, we were all lulled into a false sense of security when suddenly our serenity was shattered. "Gadzooks!" I said, looking up ahead and tooting my horn.

"Ye Gods!" said Dortha, close behind me. A solid mass of bicycles was pedaling hell-bent head-on. An elementary school had just let out, spewing forth its inmates in a river of handlebars and whirling wheels.

We were suddenly wading upstream through a noisy, chattering flood of happy young Swedes, freshly sprung from the bondage of the academic system to swirl around us in little eddies, oohing and aahing and gesticulating at the crazy foreigners on their odd-looking bikes.

"I hope the natives are friendly," said Dortha, unnerved by the proximity of the boisterous mass.

"You speak English!" said a pretty little towhead wheeling alongside, her freckles brushed by long pigtails. "You English?"

"American," said the wife, smiling at the pixie.

This triggered it. We learned that all the Scandinavian children had to take at least three years of English as a prerequisite to graduation, and they were all starved for someone to practice it on. And Americans at that! We were promptly embroiled in a loud, linguistic stew of Swedish-English.

Then instead of working our way through the throng, we found we were leading the wave of rolling, jabbering-a-mile-a-minute cacophony that had decided to ride with us. The redhead's dormant schoolteaching profession rose to the surface, and we pedaled along twelve abreast, Dortha chatting with the children, correcting grammar structure and pronunciation; Holly and Scott did the same.

Then someone burst into song, singing a somewhat garbled version of one of their English-taught lyrics—*Row, Row,*

Row Your Boat—and everyone joined in, singing at the top of their lungs. Oblivious to an oncoming car that had to seek refuge in a ditch, Dortha directed the group with nods of her head, singing out in her pretty, clear voice.

Row, Row, Row Your Boat segued into a lively Swedish song, and it was our turn to get laughed at for our bungling attempts at Swedish as we joined in, much to the amazement of passersby who surely thought Dortha was some kind of red-haired Pied Piper whisking their happy seedlings off to some never-never land.

"Scott," I called, pulling up and looking around for our official photographer. "We've got to get a picture of this." I finally spotted his lanky frame cycling way up ahead, holding hands with a precocious little towhead who was looking up at him as if he were some kind of transplanted Steve McQueen—both singing merrily along.

I paused for a moment, allowing the pumping parade to bypass me, and watched as it ascended a small rise in the road, then dipped out of sight, the sound of the musical voices trailing behind in the dust of the road.

Oh, well, I thought to myself as I started after them. No matter. Even with pictures nobody would believe it.

It was midafternoon, our escort having reluctantly peeled off one by one, and we were tooting along a narrow path that had slowly reduced from a good-sized road. It wasn't on my map, but it still went south paralleling the beach, and since our eventual destination—Landskrona—was a seaboard city, I knew we were heading in the right direction.

The path rolled out onto a beautiful greenbelt of well-manicured lawn. "Is this class?" I asked. "Is this a little hunk of beauty I've arranged?"

"This is truly classy grass," said Dortha. "Lovely."

I heard a zipping sound of something flying through the air. The missile cracked against a large tree, bounced off, and rolled up to my feet. "Great balls of fire!" I exclaimed. "Looks like a golf ball."

"Either that," said Dortha, coming to a halt behind me and staring at the object, "or one crazy hailstone."

I looked around, then spotted the triangular flag sticking up out of a nearby green. "We're on a golf course!"

"Shrewd deduction, Pop," said Scott. "That probably explains the golf carts."

"I suggest we get our fannies out of here. This could be a no-man's-land." We took off at high speed down the path, keeping a wary eye out for flying objects. The path, unfortunately, led right across the golf course, through several perplexed foursomes whose members stopped in midswing to study the interloping caravan pedaling furiously across the fairways. Stopping only once to retrieve Holly out of a sandtrap, we pulled up panting in front of the clubhouse.

"Fastest eighteen holes on record," gasped Scott.

"Hush that talk," I said. "Looks like a golf pro coming. He'll be charging us greens fees."

The golf pro accepted our apologies, and although he spoke no English, he was very lucid in his instructions on how to get the hell off his golf course. He personally escorted us to a smooth-surfaced road that took off from the clubhouse grounds and wended vaguely toward the direction we were heading. Then he bade us goodbye, talking oddly to himself and shaking his head a lot.

We started up the road—a meandering arterial that aspired more to angles vertical than horizontal. The fledglings, adroitly compensating for the incline with downshifted gears, soon left the oldsters in the dust. I stayed with Dortha and her still unsuccessful attempts at shifting her derailleur. High gears no match for the heaven-bound terrain, she alighted and we both walked up the hill pushing our bikes.

"Don't sweat it, my dear," I huffed a quarter of an hour later. "Think how much fun it'll be going down the hill."

"Let's stop a minute," she said, breathing hard, "while I think about it." We parked our bikes against a tree and sat down on a split-rail fence. "Whew! I think I'm going to expire. I wish I were in better shape."

"You're in great shape," I said, plucking a dandelion and handing it to her. "If you were in any better shape I couldn't stand it. In fact," I waggled my brows at her. "What say you and I take your great shape over to yon haystack? Play a little kissy-face?"

She looked at me out of the corner of her eye and gave my dandelion back. "Honestly! If you don't think of the darnedest thing at the darnedest times."

"Correction. I think about it all the time. I just mention it at the darnedest times."

"Just address yourself to your map, hotlips. Tell me how far we've got to go before I can check my bicycle seat for the night."

I sighed heavily and pulled out the map. "We are indeed fortunate. The road we're on happens to be on the map. Makes for much easier navigation." I checked off the mileage. "About eight clicks from here is the swinging village of Orenas. There we have reservations at a most comfortable way station."

"Reservations? How did we get reservations?"

"I got them in Hälsingborg while you people were window-shopping and making like tourists. Your old troop commander checked in at the Hälsingborg Tourist Office, consulted with a most obliging and hospitable young lady, and told her we'd like a nice place to stay about fifteen miles south. She recommended a handsome chalet at Orenas, forthwith telephoned subject hostelry and procured reservations. In doing my homework I found that nearly every town in Scandinavia has a tourist office where they are most happy to help out a tourist. Especially a tall, sexually attractive American like your husband."

"Did you say chalet? We're staying at a chalet?"

"That's what I said. Now am I or am I not one helluva troop commander?"

"You are one helluva troop commander, my dear." She pursed her lips and gave me a smack on the cheek.

"The chalet comes complete with swimming pool and sauna. You and I could adjourn to the steam room, get heated up, maybe indulge in a little plain and fancy hanky-pank——"

It's amazing how painful a shin kick can be delivered by a soft-toed tennis shoe.

We finally arrived at the crest of the long climb to find the kids stretched out under a shade tree fast asleep. Waking them, I pointed at the vista of greenery spread out below. The road dipped in a long, downhill slope to a palatial mansion surrounded by gently undulating grounds that spread clear to the shores of the sound. It was a picture plucked right out of Grimms' fairy tales.

"There, gang," I said, "is your manger for the night. What do you think of it?"

"Hey, Pops!" said Holly. "Far out! We're really going to sleep there?"

"We are."

"I dig it," said Scott. "They got a taproom?"

"Down, boy," said Dortha. "Since you turned twenty-one you think everything has to gurgle."

"That looks like nearly a two-mile run," I said. "Be sure and check your brakes. Don't go so fast you'll lose control."

Scott looked at me. "What did you say the world's bicycle speed record is?"

"According to Bobby Walthour it's one hundred and twenty-eight miles an hour."

"I'm going to break it."

"Just be sure that's all you break. Okay? Let's go!"

The kids were off like a shot and became specks in the distance before Dortha and I got under way. But once started, the same gravity that had tugged at us so relentlessly uphill made amends by shooting us down the smooth road at a lively clip. The cool breeze whipping the steam from our bodies, the toboggan thrill of close-to-the-ground speed requiring no exertion to produce, the heady good-feeling fatigue following a hard day's work—all combined to produce a loud, uncontrollable war whoop.

"*Yeeeaahooooooo!*" I roared, passing a car for the first time as we sailed around a rattling Volvo.

"*This is the life!*" yelled Dortha, hot on my heels, the wind snatching the words from her mouth.

Except for blasting through a hatch of winged insects crossing the road, and a near brush with a hay wagon that picked an inopportune time to pull onto the highway, it was a wild, wonderful, exhilarating way to wind up the day. Without pumping a single stroke, gravity propelled us right to the doorstep of the castle before petering out.

"Wow!" said Dortha, coasting up behind me. She replaced the scarf that had blown to the back of her head and flashed bug-specked teeth. "That was a thrill!"

"Now," I said, picking a straw from her hair. "Bicycling isn't all bad, is it?"

"Not all bad," she admitted. "If it could just be downhill all the way." She looked back at the long slope we had descended. Then her brows gathered. "Oh, no!"

"What is it, honey?"

"That hill! What if we have to go back up it tomorrow?"

"That's tomorrow's problem. We'll face it after we've tied on the feedbag and had a good night's rest. Let's check in."

We unloaded our bikes and took our luggage into the lobby. As I was signing in at the reception desk, I happened to look over my shoulder at the wife.

She was looking soulfully out the window at that long, steep hill.

According to the desk clerk, the baronial castle with its beautiful grounds had been the former home of a sugar plantation owner. I had trouble equating sugar plantations with Sweden, but didn't press the point as its conversion into a hotel had produced large and beautiful rooms that overlooked the magnificent landscaping lapped by the sea. I was even more delighted to learn the rate was five dollars a person.

Empty fuel tanks clamoring, we lost no time in washing up and presenting ourselves at the dining hall. We had all sprung loose our one good set of double knits, thinking the dining room guests would undoubtedly attire themselves in keeping with the formal decor of the castle. It was surprising, therefore, to find the nicely appointed salon aswim with Swedish uniforms.

"My Gad," I said. "Has war been declared?"

A tall maitre d', sweeping up in time to hear my remark, smiled. "Not really, sir. The army is here on maneuvers. They're staying at the hotel."

"Thank God for that. I left my howitzer in my bicycle bag."

"I didn't know Sweden had an army," said Dortha. "Sweden's always been neutral."

"We have a very neutral army," said the maitre d', grinning. "Would you care to come this way?"

We followed the maitre d', while the eyes of every young

soldier in the room followed Holly. "Well, Holly," I said when we were seated at a table on the terrace. "Looks like hog heaven for a sweet young thing."

"Daddy!" said Holly, taking a rare stab at insouciance.

"All I said was—*ouch!*" I turned to my wife. "I'm going to get you some carpet slippers. I'm developing a very tender shinbone."

"Your daughter is now a young lady. Treat her like one."

I looked at Holly. "Do you want me to treat you like a young lady, or like my old buddy?"

Holly reached out and patted my hand. "Both, Daddy."

"Okay, kitten. I'll try. I really will." On the pretense of burying myself in my menu, I peeked over it at my daughter. By Godfrey, she was a young lady! Dressed in a pretty pantsuit, her long blonde hair swept up in a fashionable hairdo, she was not only a lady, but a very attractive one. I dissolved a ridiculous lump in my throat with a long pull of Swedish beer.

Of course, there's that magical day when it happens to every father: when the realization suddenly hits him that the special relationship between father and daughter is to be drastically changed; when that lovable lump of freckles and peanut butter would rather sit on someone else's lap than his; when a never-separated sidekick suddenly becomes a sex symbol. It was odd, however, that it should dawn on me in an old chateau in Sweden, of all places. And in a dining room bursting with Swedish soldiers.

I noticed over my beer glass that my young lady was not oblivious to the handsome young Scandinavians around her. With a toss of her head, a feminine pat at her hair, a glance in search of the waiter, she pretty well managed to survey the field surreptitiously. I sighed, feeling a little sorry for myself. Scratch one sidekick. One lovable little buddy that would be pretty hard to replace. Maybe I should get a dog. A good hunting dog. That's it. Maybe a—

"Andy!" My musing was shattered by the distaff. "The waiter is waiting for your order."

"I think I'd like a hunting dog," I said. "Maybe a red-haired spaniel."

After dinner, Scott, Holly, and I decided to take a dip in the pool, then soak in the sauna, then dissolve into bed. Dortha reneged on the idea, not wishing to expose her black and blue torso to the outside world.

Finding it difficult to share a swimming pool with the Swedish Army, Scott and I elected to take a sauna. Holly, we noticed, had no trouble at all finding an opening in the pool.

The Swedish thermometer translated to one hundred and forty degrees, and we no sooner popped into the oven than every pore on our bodies opened with a hiss. We gingerly tested hot planks with bare bottoms, then surrendered ourselves to Nirvana.

"Well, Scott," I said, "this is the life, wot?"

"Right, Dad. The life."

I looked over at my son. My Lord, he was getting big! Six feet four inches of brawn with a disgustingly flat stomach. What the hell was happening to my offspring? This seemed to be a night for revelation. "You've been wearing a long face. Wanna talk about it?"

"It's nothing, Dad. I'm fine."

"That means women trouble. Right?"

He looked over at me, a crooked smile on his face. "Maybe a little."

"Any of my business?"

"If you want to hear about it."

"You're upset about Betty Jo not arriving in Copenhagen."

"A little. I'm just sorry she couldn't share this trip to Sweden. The better time I have, the more guilt feelings I get, and the worse I feel."

"Maybe if you'd quit enjoying yourself so much you wouldn't feel so bad."

"That's what I'll do. I'll start having a lousier time so I'll be happier."

"Good thinking." I wiped the sweat from my eyes. "Remember what Phyllis said? The nice gal from the Serendipity Travel Agency in San Berdoo who came up to help us with our trip planning?"

"Afraid I don't."

"First question she asked, when I told her you young folks were going with us, was if either of you was emotionally involved. Had a hot love affair going. She said that spoiled more trips than anything else. Instead of enjoying the wonders of Europe, too many youngsters spend the time mooning and moaning over some great, unrequited love. It can really louse up a great trip."

"I suppose so. But I'm not going to let it louse up this one. Betty Jo will be in Copenhagen by the time we get back. She'll be a definite asset to this expedition. You wait and see."

"Maybe. But I wish you were unencumbered like Holly. She's going to meet people over here. Stay wide open. Make some fine European friends. Bringing a California girl to Scandinavia is like taking Gravy Train to a banquet."

There was a firm tone to his voice. "Betty Jo would hardly be classified as dog food. No way."

"Don't construe this as casting aspersions on Betty Jo. She's a sweet kid. It's only that this is such a great opportunity to broaden your spectrum. Half the fun of seeing Europe is the people you meet. When you import your own, you miss a lot."

"Well, I've already invited her. With your concurrence. So let's change the subject. Okay?"

"Sure, son." I slapped him on the knee. "Didn't mean to harp, bucko. Just testing our new theory. Thought if I can get you feeling real bad, you might enjoy yourself more."

He grinned through beads of perspiration as I struggled to a vertical position and headed for the door. "Thanks, Dad. You really know how to cheer a fellow up."

5

A Scatological Elephant
Is a Big Problem

THE next morning we were ready to roll bright and early. Not a cloud cast a shadow on the rolling greens that smelled of early-morning dew; only the song of birds gave life to the stillness.

"So you're sure we don't have to climb that hill?" asked Dortha, relief mixing with uncertainty.

"According to the man at the desk, yonder trail leads to the beach road. To the best of his recollection, the beach road goes right to Landskrona, our destination. I'm willing to gamble."

"If it means not climbing that hill, you have a partner. Lead on, trailblazer."

"Very well." I gave the signal. "*Wagons*—HO!"

"Just a minute, Dad." I glanced back at Holly. She was looking up at the steps of the hotel, a curious light in her eyes. I followed her gaze. Bounding down the steps was a young Swedish soldier.

"I was afraid I'd missed you," he said, his accented English booming across the lawn as he approached.

"We're just leaving, Erik," said Holly. She turned to us.

"I'd like to have you meet my family. This is Erik Swenson."

Dortha and Scott acknowledged the introduction. He came over to me. I looked up at the figure towering above me with outstretched hand, and decided I'd better stand up. I was perturbed to find I *was* standing up. "Hello, Erik," I said, shaking hands and looking up at a pair of bright eyes mounted in the top of Mount Everest.

"I'm glad to meet you, Colonel Anderson." I retrieved the putty that had been four of my favorite fingers. "I had the pleasure of meeting your daughter at the pool last night. I hope you won't think I'm forward."

"With a grip like that you can be forward, guard, or jumping center. How tall are you, anyway?"

He grinned disarmingly. "It's an illusion, sir. It's these jumpboots. Very thick soles." I looked down at the remains of at least three cows. "Barefoot I'm only six feet eight."

"Oh."

"Holly told me last night she would not be averse to seeing me again. With your approval, sir, I'd like to do that."

"Well." I shot a look at my daughter. Her face was impassive but the message in her eyes came in loud and clear. "Holly's desires are my command. But who's going to run the army?"

"I have leave next week. Holly told me about your trip. I was hoping I might catch up with you. Perhaps cycle along a day or two, if you have no objection."

"You not only have my approval, young man, but you may also have a copy of our itinerary." I rummaged in the pannier, producing an extra sheet. "It's not ironclad, by any means, but we'll try to follow it as closely as we can. Leave a message at any of the mail-pickup points. We'll contact you."

"Fine. Thank you, sir." He moved over to Holly. Taking her hand he shook it firmly. "I'm looking forward to seeing you again, Holly."

"That would be nice, Erik. Good-bye."

He stood for a moment looking at her, then turned around and bounded up the steps in three strides.

When he disappeared into the lobby, Dortha turned to her daughter. "Say, Holly. He's cute."

"He's square," said Holly. "But he's nice."

"A few corners never hurt anybody," I said. "And when a man's built like the whole Green Bay Packer backfield, it's nice to know he's nice." I looked around at the troops. "We all set?" I received affirmative nods from all members of the expedition. "Very well. Let's get this medicine show on the road." I kicked off in the lead and started down the narrow trail that led to the beach road.

Halfway down it suddenly became evident the man at the desk had left out one small detail concerning the path. "S-S-S-S-STEPS!" I chattered, bobbing down the first flight that had been obscured by a tall hedge. "D-D-D-D-DON'T C-C-C-COME T-T-T-THIS W-W-WAY!"

The others heeded my warning in time to peel off and detour down the sloping lawn. I managed to stop after the first long flight, dismount, and walk down the remaining flight carrying the bike. Still vibrating, I rejoined them in the road. "Honey," asked the wife. "You all right?"

"I think your concern," I said, spitting out the remnants of a good cigar, "might be more sincere if you'd quit giggling."

"I'm sorry," she said, covering her mouth. "But you did make quite a picture."

"That's all I needed on a posterior already tender. Banging down eighty-five cement steps. Now that we've had our little laugh for the day we'll organize a search party to find my fillings."

In spite of the early morning contretemps, it was an exhilarating ride on the beach road that unreeled along the Swedish coastline. The sound was clear as crystal, the shoreline bedecked with graceful swans, the little houses in the fishing villages ablaze with flowers of every hue. The Swedes take full advantage of their summers by adorning them with every type of blossom imaginable. Dortha was in seventh heaven, even forgetting the tender epidermis that enfolded her bicycle seat, as she wheeled along marveling at the flora and fauna abounding everywhere.

We didn't even mind too much when midmorning found us running out of paved road and onto a dirt road, which in turn petered out to nothing but rocky beach. We dismounted, laboriously pushing our cycles through the deep sand until we came to a couple of fishermen. They obligingly directed us to the nearest road leading to Landskrona.

We puffed up several fairly steep hills, through pastoral farmlands inhabited by grazing cows fat with the milk that produced Sweden's world-famous cheeses and dairy products. During our frequent rest stops we had ample opportunity to absorb the *real* agrarian life, visiting with the grassroots people who form the backbone of Sweden's awe-inspiring kingdom. At one point, following a hot and thirsty climb, we were invited to enjoy huge glasses of cold, fresh milk in the immaculate home of a dairyman.

Late in the morning we pulled up to a fork in the road that posed a definite enigma. The two branches took off to meander over the pastureland and disappear in opposite directions. The wrong road could take us far out of our way. Since neither was on the map, we had no way of knowing which was the right road. It had just come to the flip-a-coin stage when we observed a motorcycle bearing down on us.

I hailed the driver, who dutifully skidded to a halt. I approached the young cyclist, map in hand. After several tries, my best efforts to communicate were rewarded with nothing more than shrugged shoulders and a helpless look of apology. I was just at the point of thanking him and sending him on his way when Dortha stepped up.

She made several motions, gesticulating with her fingers, and suddenly a light came on in the young man's eyes. The cyclist pointed animatedly at the right fork of the road, and nodded his head vigorously. There were several more finger exercises, then he kicked his machine into life and went roaring down the road, waving until swallowed by a plume of dust.

"That's the road we want," said Dortha, pointing to the right fork. She climbed back on her bicycle.

I looked at my wife in awe. "How did you communicate with that young buck? I couldn't get him to understand a word."

She gave me a solemn look. "Simple. The young man is deaf."

"Go on!"

"Have you forgotten your old wife used to teach the deaf? I recognized the problem immediately."

"But what—how did you communi——"

"Elementary, my dear Watson. By the deaf sign language. It sometimes transcends language barriers. Now, if there are no further questions, I suggest we be on our way. Didn't you want to make Landskrona before lunch?" She started down the road, turning at the right fork.

I just stood and watched her for a moment, my jaw swinging on its hinge. Then I jumped on my bicycle, and pedaled hard to catch up. "How the hell," I muttered to myself, "did Brigham Young ever find Salt Lake City without Big Red?"

We glided down a long hill and onto the cobblestone streets of Landskrona. The ingratiating town became even more endearing by its provision of cycle paths along its bustling city streets.

Dusty and thirsty, we pulled into the first outdoor café to

refresh ourselves. Scott had picked up a hacking cough, which he tried to keep at arm's length with a vile Swedish substitute for Alka-Seltzer called "Samarin," by pouring the stuff into everything he drank. When our refreshments arrived, Scott poured the medication into his orange juice, which promptly began fizzing all over the place.

I knew what was coming next, and looked around to see how many people were watching. Happily, the café was nearly deserted as Scott went into his Dr. Jekyll routine with the foaming libation. He drank it, then turned into Mr. Hyde with slurping facial contortions and hair-sprouting histrionics that would have made Spencer Tracy turn in his SAG card.

I finally found the elderly proprietress hiding behind the counter, coaxed her out long enough to settle the check (I had learned never to attempt an explanation), then herded Mr. Hyde onto his bicycle and we escorted him through town to the ferry that was to take us back to Denmark.

It's not always easy running a crack wagon train.

All too soon we were leaving Sweden. We had nibbled just a canapé of this great smorgasbordian country. Just a tantalizing tidbit that made us desire more of what Sweden had to offer. The gracious, friendly people; the exquisite Swedish products; the quaint yet ultramodern shops; the grandeur of unspent nature—they all beckoned us to return for a longer stay. I marked it on my mental calendar to do just that as we wheeled our bikes into the cavernous tunnel of the gleaming Swedish ferry.

We went topside for a bite of lunch. I knew the moment we walked into the spacious dining room and passed the smorgasbord table that I was in for trouble. Never had I seen such an array of saliva-pumping comestibles as presented themselves in silver-trayed splendor on the long, white tablecloth. Every manner of fish, fowl, and four-foot was prepared in a dozen different ways, designed to set the hunger pangs to palpitating, the taste buds to blossoming.

And they succeeded.

"Dad!" said Scott, as we sat down at a nearby table. "Did you see what I just saw?"

"I saw it," I said. "Don't forget you're a sick man. Holly, pull out the jam sandwiches you swiped at breakfast."

"Did you ever in your life see such a buffet?" asked the wife. "Look at that cold lobster."

"Jam or marmalade sandwich?" I asked.

"Daddy," said Holly, "isn't that caviar in that silver dish?"

"Would you care for tea or coffee with your sandwiches?"

"I could eat a horse," said Scott. "I've never been so hungry in my life."

"Quit drooling on your sister," I said, "and eat your sandwich." I made the mistake of looking over at the wife. She was appealing to me through eyes stolen from a basset hound. I knew I was sunk before she said it.

"Honey, the kids haven't had an honest-to-goodness smorgasbord since they've been in Scandinavia. They should have at least one. Maybe this would be a good time. You and I can eat the sandwiches."

I looked at Holly. She had the back of her hand to her brow, obviously on the brink of fainting from hunger. "Never mind, Dad," she said stoically. "I think I'm too weak to make it to the buffet."

I looked at Scott. He was gnawing on the tablecloth.

I looked up at the waiter who had materialized at our table. My silent request for help went unheeded. Resigning myself, I said, "If we can sell our bicycles, I think we can afford the smorgasbord for two." I addressed the troops. "You have exactly seventy minutes until this restaurant pulls into Copenhagen. I want you to get your money's worth. Now. On your mark, get set, *Go!*"

I'd seen slower scrambles for a red-red alert. For the next hour and ten minutes the wife and I gnawed cold sandwiches (I hate marmalade) accompanied with the aroma of cold lobster, broasted chicken, sliced tenderloin, pâté de foie gras, and caviar. We watched—as in a time-lapse movie—the annihilation of a beautiful buffet spread. Under the expert tutelage of the Swedish waiter, the guests were instructed in the fine art of smorgasbording: always start with fish, leave the dirty plate at your table, pick up a clean one for each succeeding course (the waiter worked up a lather just removing the dirty dishes). When in doubt about what accessories go with a main dish, select from the condiments placed around it. Tackle the cold dishes first, work up to the hot ones.

When Scott returned from his first foraging expedition with a heaping plate of smoked herring, the waiter stopped him with a flashed palm. "One would not think of eating herring without a glass of aquavit," he issued in stentorian tones. "It is against all gastronomic rules." So saying, he visited the bar to return with two brimming glasses of legalizing amber liquid.

"By all means," I said, shuddering at the thought of what all this was going to cost. "Let's not violate any gastronomic rules." One also, of course, has to have three different wines, since to drink the same wine with fish as one did with meat or fowl was the most gross type of barbarism. And to finish the meal without coffee and brandy was like a kiss without a goatee.

The *kinder* finally descended on the dessert table, and we watched heaping dishes of fresh fruit compote smothered in whipped cream dissolve, while we polished off our bread crusts. "Never dreamed a bike required so much fuel," I said. "Next time we'll take a Rolls-Royce. Cheaper."

When finally the boat nudged the pier at Copenhagen, Dortha and I helped our two still-munching offspring out of their chairs. I went over to the waiter to try and make restitution for the damages wrought—wondering if they'd accept my American war bonds—and steeled myself for the check. The waiter was most gracious, delivering the document on a silver tray. Gingerly picking it up and peeking at the total out of the corner of my eye, I was dumbstruck. Long acquainted with the escalated prices charged by train diners and shipboard restaurants, I was hardly prepared for this.

The total—counting wine, liquor, the works—came to less than six dollars.

Maybe it was the taxless freedom of the high seas. Maybe it was the benevolence of a waiter who had a thing for starving Americans. Whatever it was, it's a strange dichotomy that the Swedes charge a buck twenty for a pack of cigarettes, yet deliver a repast fit for a king—including spirits—for under three dollars.

I don't know which the waiter appreciated more: the nice tip I left him, or the juicy smack on the forehead.

We landed at Copenhagen's Tuborg Harbor, home of the incomparable Tuborg beer, and cycled through the scrubbed-clean brewery. Scott dragged his heels all the way, noisily extolling the virtues of checking the taproom. Realizing the pitfalls awaiting our ride through Copenhagen in a sober condition, much less trying to match wits with Danish drivers with several flagons of stout Danish beer aslosh in our midriffs, I vetoed the idea. Besides, I had no intention of getting arrested for drunken bike driving. So subscribing to prudence, instead of tracking down the taproom, we chased down a telephone to locate a room for the night.

Unhappily, Meta Jensen was all filled up. Again consulting Frommer's book, I tried several small hotels until finally finding room at the Du Nord hotel near the train station. This meant driving through downtown Copenhagen; Dortha, feeling a bit more confident on her bike, confirmed she could handle it. Saddlesore but more attuned to traffic, we reached the hotel with only one minor incident. It was I, this time, who was the victim.

I was brushed by a young man in a delivery truck who was busier watching Holly up ahead than the old poop on his right flank. Instead of falling, however, I ricocheted neatly off a flower cart and kept right on going. Proving Danes may have malice in their heart, but compassion in their souls, I again met up with my assailant farther down the street. He had circled several blocks to catch up with me and ascertain my well-being. I was only sorry he had to knock off my rear reflector the second time he came around to apologize for hitting me the first time.

The Du Nord Hotel ($5.50 per person, including breakfast) was an interesting if not auspicious pension in what proved to be the seamy part of Copenhagen, just a block from the train station. The obliging clerk helped us store our cycles in a dungeon under the building, then escorted us to our room— a huge, high-domed garret with dormer windows that afforded an excellent view of the pornographic bookstore across the street.

Too tired to dress for dinner, Dortha volunteered to go downstairs to a delicatessen and bring some cold victuals up to the room. We spent an edifying, if not particularly inspiring, evening eating cold chicken and potato salad and watching the pornographic shop below. It seemed to be the main place for business for Ladies of the Evening hawking their wares to Men of the Hour. Fearing the morals of the youngsters would be corrupted by exposure to such commercial conduct, the wife tried every ruse to interest them in other activities. Finally realizing her labors would be more fruitful trying to move Mount Rushmore, she gave up and joined us at the window.

It was she, in fact, who directed our attention to the well-dressed man who was in a heated debate with an attractive lady of easy virtue. The words were inaudible, but the actions were unmistakable. The young man was waving his Master Charge card around and shouting profanities at the high-heeled practitioner of the world's oldest profession, who insisted on ignoring the financial trappings of the twentieth century: she would not accept his credit card. As we watched the outcome with bated breath, it was the woman, as usual, who solved the problem. They eventually headed down the street, hand in hand. Only his wristwatch was now on her wrist.

"Love will find a way," I said. "Isn't that beautiful?"

"Really inspirational," said the better half. "Now how about you voyeurs pulling the shade and coming to bed?"

Reluctantly we shelved further studies of Copenhagen's intriguing morality, and climbed into the sack. To be lulled to sleep by the *wee-wah-wee-wah-wee-wah* of wailing police cars.

The next morning, over our continental breakfast in the hotel's tiny dining room, we discussed the shakedown cruise. I had been reluctant to mention it, as Dortha was still applying makeup with a butter knife to cover up her psychedelic coloring, and was still limping slightly from her sprained knee. I was agreeably surprised, therefore, to find enthusiastic unanimity on the success of our trial trip to Sweden. It proved to have reaped far more pleasures than problems. In spite of the fact the oldsters had not really mastered the tricky talent of smoothly shifting gears (Dortha had spent nearly all the trip plodding along in high gear), and the older generation's behinds still puckered at the sight of a bicycle seat, we were all looking forward to getting on with the real trip.

After breakfast, in high spirits, we cycled over and presented our machines to Mr. Norit for a final checkup. The proprietor seemed very pleased, if a little surprised, to see us again, and promptly set to work tightening cables, greasing sprockets, and securing loose nuts. We were to pick up the bikes the following morning.

Striking out on foot we dropped by the American Express Office to check the mail. As we were to discover throughout the trip, this was a frustrating, unpleasant task. One had to wade through a cordon of long-haired, often rank-smelling young people—predominantly Americans—who, for some reason, refused to let a dead cult rest in peace, and continued to flaunt the hippy uniform of beads, sandals, fringes, and cast-off military clothing. As if their appearance wasn't enough to gag a maggot off a gut wagon, these let-it-all-hang-out refugees accosted passersby with every manner of article for sale—from junk jewelery to secondhand buses—presumably to scrape up enough money to get back home. Standing in a long mail line, we were to witness natives cross a busy street just to walk on the other side and avoid the flotsam that surrounded the American Express Office. In short, it was a bad scene. A lousy thing to do to someone else's country.

And the American Express Company officials, admittedly plagued with problems above and beyond the pale, alas, had not risen to the challenge. Picking up the mail could require standing in line for hours, only to be greeted by surly and snarling clerks. Trying to get tourist information was virtually impossible; and we found even the American Express conducted tours were not up to standard.

Virtually anyone who can afford traveler's checks can also get a check guarantee card, or letter of credit from their Stateside bank. Bank services abroad are just as accommodating as those in the States, if not more so. Armed with a Bank of America courtesy card, we had little trouble cashing checks anywhere. And with the increasingly broad acceptance of American credit cards, we found the financial aspects of our journey the least of our problems.

For future trips abroad we vowed to use the local post office general delivery for our mail (you have to go to the post office anyway to get stamps), let our banker handle our financial affairs (banks will even provide foreign currency kits to expedite your arrival), and utilize the excellent and very accommodating native tourist offices throughout Europe (that bend over backward to assist in your tourist needs).

Among our mail was a letter for Scott from Betty Jo. For some reason her charter flight would not be arriving in Copenhagen until the following week. Adjourning to a local tearoom, we set about trying to lift the long face on our number one son. I wasn't doing a very good job, not being at all sympathetic with Scott's project of bringing coals to Newcastle. I imprudently slipped into a father's I-told-you-so role. Things were going from bad to worse, until the redhead finally stepped in.

"Now, both of you quit glaring at each other," said my roommate, who should have been head of the United Nations. "Betty Jo is on her way. There's nothing we can do about that. And if Scott wants her here, there's nothing we *should* do. So. I suggest Scott stay here to meet her. The rest of us can stick to our itinerary, then when Betty Jo arrives, she and Scott can catch the train and join us. Anything wrong with that idea?"

Scott's face brightened. "Sounds good to me. I can stay here at one of the hostels. Then I can meet her plane. No one should come to this great city and not be met." He looked at me. "What do you say, Dad?"

"I don't like busting up the family for a week. We were all going to make this journey together. Maybe the last one we'll ever take as a family—just the four of us." I reached for my handkerchief and wiped my nose. "With all my little fledglings leaving the nest—"

I suffered a gouge in the ribs from the distaff. "Knock it off, you ham. You know how far you get with that routine."

"Cool it, Pop," said Holly. "Jimmy Stewart you aint. Now admit it's a good idea."

"It used to work for Judge Hardy," I said, replacing my handkerchief.

"Who's Judge Hardy?"

"Never mind." I looked at my son. "I don't like it. But if I go along with the idea, will you take the ground glass out of my tea?"

"You bet." He switched his cup with mine. "Peace, Father?"

"An uneasy truce. Now you'll need money for the train trip. You can meet us in Amsterdam. You'll need dough to live on. Figure what it's going to cost. I'll cash a check."

I received a look with no daggers. "Thanks, Dad."

Holly put her arm around my neck. "You may not be Jimmy Stewart, but for a father you're not all bad." She kissed my cheek.

"Thanks, kitten. I needed that."

It was our plan to pick up the bikes and shove off the first thing next morning, so the rest of the afternoon was spent in preparation. Scott and Holly went sight-seeing (to the zoo, of all places), Big Red repaired to the laundromat to refresh the fabrics, and I journeyed to the bank to pump up my money belt. We all met for dinner at an inexpensive but delicious family restaurant called the Lido on Vesterbrogade Street. Then I made a proposition I was sure would be hard to sell.

Among the many delights of Copenhagen is a circus that plays all summer long, smack in the center of town. Tickets are very inexpensive (starting at a buck), and there's no such thing as a bad seat, since they're all practically in the arena. As an old circus buff from the year one, I knew this world-renowned big top drew the finest acts in Europe.

As predicted, my suggestion that we all go to the circus was met by a resounding endorsement of ho-hums. "Nevertheless," I said, undaunted, "*I'm* going to the circus. If anyone else wants to come, fine." So saying, I bought a bag of peanuts and set out for the amphitheater. I ended up buying four seats.

The Copenhagen Circus has to be the biggest entertainment bang for the buck in the show-biz world. Great acts, music, costuming, clowns, animals, high wire, trapeze performers—everything. And for a finale, the arena floor rolls back to disclose a huge pool and a splendid aquatic act, followed by a colorful, splashing spectacular of singing fountains. Transported back to the age of prepill innocence, we all giggled, gasped, and guffawed with unabashed exuberance.

The only flaw marring the evening performance was caused by a diabolical elephant. He had no sooner put his foot on the heaving chest of the pretty, supine blonde, than he decided to vent his views on show business. He opened all valves. Simultaneously. Needless to say, this caused something of a stir, particularly on behalf of the prostrate young lady lying under the elephant. It was not surprising, therefore, that an ad appeared in the "Help Wanted" column of the paper the next morning, soliciting for a pretty blonde who wanted to break into show business.

On our way back to the hotel the troops grudgingly admitted they had enjoyed the evening as much as I. As we crawled into bed, still yakking about the circus, I noticed the accustomed *wee-wah-wee-wah* wail of the police cars was interspersed with the throaty roar of fire trucks. Rising to assure myself that our hotel wasn't being consumed by flames, I satisfied myself it wasn't, and went back to bed to fall into deep slumber. And enjoy marvelous dreams of owning my own scatological elephant that accompanied me on story meetings with movie producers and book editors.

I awoke the next morning still wearing a wraparound

smile, and it didn't even disappear when I learned the fire engines we had heard in the night had been summoned to the
Lido restaurant—where we had dined the previous evening.

I indulged in a few moments of idle contemplation, wondering just what it was about the Anderson family's presence
that evoked ferry boats to crash into waiting rooms, restaurants
to blossom into flame, and elephants to do no-no's on pretty
blondes. But not being a devout believer in the occult, ESP,
or the metaphysical, I finally chalked it up to coincidence and
addressed myself to the more paramount problems at hand.

Like how do you cross the Zuider Zee on bicycles?

6

General Patton,
Look to Your Laurels!

IT was Sunday morning. Traffic was sparse as we headed south through Copenhagen. Grumbling skies matched our mood as we bade farewell to Scott, who accompanied us to the city limits, then turned back, looking very forlorn, his long legs pumping dejectedly. I kept my thoughts to myself, but hated the circumstances that had separated the family. My travel agent was right. Kids should leave emotional hang-ups at home when traveling abroad.

As the three of us spun along on a nice cycling road that paralleled A-2, the sun finally broke through, and by the time we stopped for our first coffee break our spirits had followed suit. Mr. Norit had done a superlative job on the bicycles; with cables tuned like a Stradivarius, chains gliding silently over well-lubricated sprockets, they whisked along effortlessly.

Refreshed, we again took to the path. It was our intention to make the little town of Köge, an easy thirty-mile trip from Copenhagen. We stopped for lunch at an outdoor café, ordering steaming cups of delicious hot chocolate with which we

90

launched sandwiches purloined from our continental breakfast. We were making good time, thanks to Denmark's foresight of making well-engineered bicycle paths an integral part of highway construction. Toward midafternoon we found ourselves on a deserted stretch of straight roadway. I pulled up alongside Dortha. "This is a good time to practice changing gears," I said. "We've got the road to ourselves. Okay?"

Reluctantly she agreed. We rode along side by side, as I tried to teach her the fundamentals of the tricky gearshifts. This proved not the easiest task in the world, as I had not completely mastered the technique myself. The mechanism for gear changing on most ten-speeds consists of two small levers positioned on the frame just under the handlebars. The left lever guides the chain on the double front chain wheel, the right lever doing likewise on the five-sprocketed rear wheel. Proper coordination of the two levers enables the rider to select any one of ten speeds desired. There are no audible clicks and no position indicators to tell which gear you are slipping into or out of. It's all done by a delicate feel, which takes practice and experience to master. Particularly as it involves removing one hand from the handlebars to manipulate the levers. Once learned, however, it becomes as automatic and easy as shifting gears on a car with a manual transmission. It's the learning part that's tricky.

Timing is also important. Upcoming deviations in the terrain have to be anticipated, and shifting accomplished when there is comparatively little strain on the bicycle chain. Properly done, an old pro can literally flow up a hill, compensating for the slope as he goes, shifting up or down in one smooth, gliding operation. This is when cycling truly becomes a joyful form of transportation. It was the tyros like us—who broke rhythm by trying one frantic gear change partway up the hill—who ended up pushing bicycles up mountains. This is easy on bicycle tires, but very tough on shoe leather and dispositions.

We rode along together, practicing shifting techniques on the level terrain. Dortha, quick to grasp things, was beginning to get the feel of it, to recognize the delicate pressures required to summon the desired gear. Her improvement was also due to becoming used to the bike and being able to relax the throttling grip she held on the handlebars. "Honey, you're doing great," I said, as she executed a neat, smooth transition. "You're getting the hang of it."

"Pshaw," she said, trying to register a nonchalance she didn't feel. "You're just saying that."

"We're coming to a little rise. I want to see you zoom right up it."

"Here goes." She zoomed right up it, but not in the manner prescribed by bicycle manuals. Just as she shifted gears, I heard the sound of a motorbike snoring up behind us. I made the mistake of crowding over on her side to allow it to pass. This spooked the redhead, who fiddling with the shift lever, had only one hand on her handlebars. Before she could regain control she had come in contact with her old nemesis—the curb! "Here I go again!" she yelled.

And she did.

Launching smoothly over the handlebars.

I reached for her, but too late. I was again confronted with the chilling sight of my beloved embracing the macadam. "Oh, dear God! Not again!" By the time I reached her, she was struggling to a sitting position. "Oh, honey!" I took her face in my hands. "Sweetheart! I spooked you!"

She looked up from a cursory examination of a scraped palm. "Darned if you didn't." And then she started laughing. "You *sure* I'm getting the hang of it?"

Vastly relieved at hearing laughter instead of moaning, I helped her to her feet and held her in my arms. "*I* did it to you. Me. Your very own loving husband. Drove you right into the curb. Can you walk?"

"Better than I can ride." She looked down at a rip in the knee of her pantsuit. "I don't mind bruising the bod, but I'm sure playing hob with my wardrobe."

"Clothes we can patch. Are *you* all right?"

"Fine. Please check my bicycle."

It was undamaged. I watched her painfully throw her leg over. "We should have gotten you a girl's bike. I don't think you'd have nearly so much trouble."

"I'm beginning to think we should have gotten me a wheelchair." She fixed her green eyes on me. "You didn't take out a big, fat life insurance policy on me, by any chance? Just before we started this trip?"

"Afraid not."

"The thought occurred. So if you're really not ready to do your old lady in, from now on we ride single file. Like the Indians. Okay?"

"Single file. Like the Indians." I noticed a flicker of pain cross her face as she settled into her seat. "You sure you feel like going on?"

"Of course."

I reached over and put my hand on hers. "Did I ever tell you I think you're one hell of a good sport?"

"Why, no, dear. Tell me I'm one hell of a good sport."

"You are. And you know what else?"

"What else, love?"

"Maybe you haven't really mastered the ten-speed yet. But your dives are certainly improving. That last swan over the handlebars was a ten-point dive if ever I saw one."

"That's nice to know, dear. You've made my day."

It was a short, one-blister ride on to Köge, which we managed with no further calamities. Having been advised that Denmark's tourist offices were usually located near the train station, we followed the tracks until we came to the depot. Sure

enough, right across the street from the depot was a tourist office. "Well, Holly," I said, leaning my bike up against a lamp
post, "the old trailblazer has done it again. Led us right to the
tourist office."

"Great navigation, old trailblazer," she replied. "Too bad
it's closed."

And, being Sunday, it was. Undeterred, I whipped out my
handy copy of *Hotels, Pensions, Inns and Motels of Denmark,*
an excellent publication put out by the Danish Tourist Bureau,
and looked for a telephone. There was a booth right across the
street from the tourist office.

According to the directory, the Hotel Hafnia was recommended and reasonable. I dialed. A gentleman answered the
phone, switched to perfect English, and advised me he could
handle a party of three for five dollars apiece, including "moms,"
service, and breakfast. Yes, he certainly could handle three bicycles. I told him to hold the reservations for me, I was on my
way.

"We have reservations at the Hotel Hafnia," I said, swinging out of the booth. "Let's hope we can find it before it gets
dark."

"This shouldn't pose too large a problem," said the wife,
pointing up at a sign above the phone booth which read Hotel
Hafnia. I presented myself at the reception desk, looking somewhat sheepish, twenty seconds later.

"Mr. Anderson?" said the proprietor, glancing up and
smiling. "What kept you?"

"Headwinds."

He chuckled. "You Americans! Who else in the whole
wide world would think of jet-propelled bicycles?"

Settled in a very nice, immaculate room, I went down to
have a drink while the women freshened up. Mr. Mortensen,
the owner of the hotel, joined me in a brandy. He turned out to
be an extremely erudite, polished gentleman who had an ex-

cellent command of English and of the situation. Obviously as interested in talking to an American as I was to a Dane, several empty brandy glasses accumulated as we discussed the future of Denmark, its tremendously high tax structure (an automobile, for instance, costing again its basic price in taxes) and whether Denmark's superb socialistic program was really worth the candle.

We were joined by his daughter, an attractive girl in her late teens, and again I was sorry Scott was not with us. Mary Ann Mortensen could have been a high-fashion model, but instead was going to school to learn to become a midwife—a career I thought had gone out with the celluloid collar. She had a beautiful blonde baby but no husband, a fact that raised nary an eyebrow in permissive Denmark.

Joined by the ladies, we moved to the dining room, surprised to find our bikes had been brought here for safekeeping. We were served huge platters of delicious plaice cooked in lemon butter, a culinary delight that would have thrilled a gourmet's gourmet. Then on up to bed, to find a cornucopic bowl of fresh fruit in our room, compliments of the manager.

If ever I'm deported from my native land, it will be on Denmark's door that I shall first knock.

My redhead seldom complained. But action speaking louder than words, her actions were speaking volumes as she got out of bed the following morning. Her latest tumble had taken more of a toll than either of us thought, and she was limping from a swollen ankle as she puttered around putting on her face. "Honey," I asked, "are you sure you feel all right?"

"Fine. Just a little stiff."

"Redhead speak with forked tongue. Lips say yes, eyes say no."

"I'll be fine as soon as we get going. I'll work out the soreness."

"I have a better idea. From the looks of the weather, it just might rain. Since we're right across the street from the depot, we're going to take the train. See how it works as a sag wagon. Give you a day off. A chance to mend."

She perked up. "Really? I can certainly bike, you know."

"I know. You're a great trouper. But you've earned a vacation. We'll just take the train to Vordingborg, about sixty kilometers down the road."

"Well, if you insist."

When we checked out, Mr. Mortensen personally insisted that he walk us to the depot, taking Dortha's bike. He helped us check them in at the baggage room, interpreting for us with the baggage man, then assisting in buying our tickets. Bidding the farewell of old friends, we said good-bye. As the train pulled in, Mary Ann came running up with two beautiful roses, one for each of the ladies. I settled happily for a kiss on the cheek, and decided right there and then that Köge would be a great place to spend a century or two.

It was a very pleasant ride through the lush lowlands. The train was a local, considerably off the beaten path, and we had a compartment to ourselves. I was just settling back, shoes off, enjoying the scenery, when the conductor popped into our compartment. Speaking no English, and quickly realizing we were strangers to the Danish tongue, he pointed to our baggage, to us, to the door, and held up two fingers. Then he departed.

"What's that all about?" asked the wife.

"I haven't the foggiest." We pulled into a train station and stopped. I was wondering why most people were getting off, when the conductor came barging in again, looking harried. He picked up our baggage, motioned for us to follow, and departed down the vestibule. We followed, I hopping along like a one-legged kangaroo trying to get my shoes on. We were no sooner unceremoniously off-loaded than the train started up.

"This isn't Vordingborg," I said astutely, staring at a station sign that read Næstved.

"When you get your shoes on," said the wife, looking grim, "maybe you'd better check at the station."

"Two fingers. The conductor held up two fingers. There's a clue there." Stamping my shoes on, I looked around the station. My eyes fell on a big cardinal "2" sign near one of the tracks. "Aha! I bet we change to track number two. And look! A train is just pulling in."

"I suggest, Sherlock Holmes, you corroborate your deduction with the ticket office. I'm not dressed for Helsinki or Minsk."

I checked. The man at the ticket office spoke no English, but a cherubic nun standing by did. She saved three souls that day.

The train for Vordingborg left at two o'clock. On track four.

From this incident we learned several things:

(1) bicycles are smarter than people, because they made the train change with no difficulty;

(2) any American who says communication in Europe is no problem is either a multilinguist or spends all his time at American embassies;

(3) in the event the people in the ticket office don't speak English—which is often the case in smaller towns—the people in the tourist offices will be happy to help.

But above all, I vowed to find out the train schedule, the track number, the transfers enroute, and all other pertinent data *before* getting on the train. Anyone who relies on assistance from English-speaking personnel on board European railroads will have more trouble with trains than Casey Jones.

"Just out of curiosity," said the wife, as we sailed along enjoying the thirty-minute ride to Vordingborg, "where would we be heading if we'd taken the train on track number two?"

"It might have been a very interesting experience," I said. "Haven't you ever had a burning desire to see Warsaw?"

Strategically located on the southern tip of Jutland, the Danish town of Vordingborg is noted primarily for its Goose Tower. This seven-storied monument marks the remains of King Valdemar Atterdag's royal fortress that was built during the fourteenth century, and became the greatest castle and fortress in the Nordic countries. It is also noted for its Prince Jorgen's Guard of forty bandsmen, ten boy pipers, and twenty guardsmen who parade around clad in true copies of the first Danish uniform, complete with original halberds and sabres.

Neither of these hallmarks was in evidence as we pulled into the train station. But as we debarked and walked back to the baggage car to claim our bicycles, we found something that proved every bit as interesting. A very high Danish lady—high not by virtue of birth, but by virtue of aquavit—noisily joined us to reclaim her possession from the baggage car. The doors opened, the baggage man handed down our bicycles, and then returned with the belongings of the elevated woman.

It was her husband. The carefree gentleman obviously had partaken of the grape a bit too freely to please fellow passengers, so rather than throw him off the train, an imaginative conductor had solved the problem by the simple expedient of tagging him and exiling him to the baggage car. Here he continued to his destination, his jubilation not disturbing the less easily offended mail sacks.

Clapping and singing as he was lifted to the ground by the baggage man, the bibacious Dane threw an arm around Holly and started marching her down the platform. The gentleman's mate forthwith corrected this faux pas with the help of a swinging umbrella; then the man and wife took off, jigging and clapping their hands in gleeful reunion.

"Darn," said Holly, laughing. "Almost had a good thing going there 'til his wife showed up."

"That's a beautiful picture," said Dortha, watching them wobbling toward the nearest saloon.

"These Danes are ingenious," I said. "It's not easy flying in a baggage car."

We hopped on our bikes and located the nearby tourist office. A lovely lady answered our query as to the available accommodations to be found for the night in Vordingborg. "We have several hotels here at various prices. But how do you feel about staying at a private home?"

"Love it," said the distaff.

"Then by all means go to Ellen Christiansen's house. She loves Americans, and her home is a neat, clean place. I always try to send nice people there."

"Thank you for making an exception," I said. "Could you call her for us?"

"Sorry. She has no phone. Just go on over." She gave us detailed instructions on how to get there, and off we went.

We cycled through the homey little town, stopped to inspect the Goose Tower, then continued toward the outskirts where Ellen Christiansen lived. I was in the lead, whistling gaily along, when I heard a distracting noise. A low, rumbling sound, almost like thunder. I looked up at the sky. It was overcast but behaving itself. I looked back. What I saw was not behaving itself. I was looking into the mouth of a very large cannon. Furthermore, the cannon was attached to a very large tank. I swallowed my gum when I saw its very large treads were just about to gnaw on my very small rear fender.

Tabling for future debate the legal right-of-way of tank versus bicycle, I lost little time in curbing my bicycle. Sucking in my stomach as the machine grumbled by, I saw the metal behemoth was not a loner. Instead, it was the vanguard of a long column of clanking monsters industriously chewing up the road behind as far as I could see. What was our lot that we should keep coming afoul of the military?

Then my heart plummeted. My next-of-kin were somewhere back in that churning parade of destruction. I was at the point of leaping on my bike and charging to the rescue, when through the dust I spotted Holly. Fifty yards behind me, she was leaning against a lamppost like some transplanted Lili Marlene, waving at the soldiers. And then the curtain of dust parted far enough to disclose my wife, a block and a half away. Even from this distance I could see that the expression on her face was definitely not pleasant. And she was in the act of doing the very thing she should not, under any circumstance, be doing.

I could imagine all too vividly the reaction of my roommate, who got spooked by auto horns, when she looked back to see the first tank snapping at her taillight. She had undoubtedly headed for the curb—hopefully not going fast enough to capsize. And not wanting to get too far behind, she had tried again, only to be beached by the second tank. Now, before my horrified eyes, she was again launching from the curb, directly in front of the third charging juggernaut.

Knowing my yells would be drowned in the rumble, and that I couldn't possibly reach her side before the armored vehicle did, I could only watch in mute terror. The tank seemed almost upon her, and then with untold relief I saw her wobble to the curb just as it clawed by. Dear God! I wiped away sweat puddled on my forehead. Now surely she'll stay put until the remainder of the column goes by.

But in my assumption I had not taken into account the strain of Irish that lies comatose under the wife's good disposition. I should have. One can push a redhead just so far. Big Red had obviously been pushed too far three different times.

And into the curb at that. As I watched, I again froze in horror.

Instead of climbing up on the sidewalk and staying there, she leaned her bike against the curb. Then she advanced into the middle of the street! Methodically she rolled up her sleeves, spread her legs, and planted herself, hands on hips, directly in the path of tank number four.

"*Dortha!*" I yelled. "*Get the hell out of the street!*" Had my voice risen above the din of the convoy, it would have fallen on deaf ears. Fearing to look, yet unable to turn away, I could only stand frozen, listening to my heart hammer my head. My depth perception warped by distance; I could have sworn the tank was already upon her, when I saw her right hand shoot out from her hip, palm forward in a stopping motion. She presented the incongruous picture of a redhaired Benito Mussolini.

And then a hand shot skyward from the tankman riding behind the gun turret. I was sure my wife was going to be macerated into dogfood, when the treads ground to a halt. The hands of following tank commanders shot up in succession along the length of the convoy. The rumble of treads was replaced by the quieter cacophony of clutched engines.

I exhaled. The wife, possessing more courage than I, had decided this *was* the time to debate the legal right-of-way of tank versus bicycle. I watched, my mouth catching flies, as the turret gunner was joined on top by the tank commander. Before either had a chance to say anything, the spouse was telling them in no uncertain terms—complete with shocking gesticulations—what she thought of tanks, military maneuvers, noisy machinery, and drivers who hogged the road.

I stood there, my adrenalin draining, my fear slowly changing to admiration, as I watched my irate, freckled David thoroughly dress down the mighty Goliath. The mechanized cavalrymen could only stare in mute bewilderment at the woman in the middle of the road whose words were strange, but whose dactyl displays certainly were not. Finally, having vented her fury, she walked over to the curb, picked up her bicycle, returned to the middle of the street, and as calm as you please, remounted. Then, once under way, she motioned it was all right to follow. At a respectable distance.

My soulmate proceeded to lead the pride of the Danish tank corps up the street. The sidewalks were lined with people, attracted by the display of military might that had chanced upon their thoroughfare as an avenue to a mock battle somewhere in defense of Denmark's coastline. Most had witnessed the spectacle of the bicycle-tank confrontation, and as Dortha passed, a rousing cheer went up along the line of march. She ignored the applauding onlookers, looking neither to the right nor to the left until she wheeled up to where I was standing at the intersection.

Once again her hand shot up. Once again the column clanged to a halt. "Isn't this where we turn to the Christiansen street?" she asked me.

"This is where we turn, General Patton."

"Very good." Holly joined us and we three crossed to the intersecting street. Safely out of harm's way, Dortha motioned for the tank commander to proceed. "You may go on to your little war. But do be more careful."

The turret gunner bowed at the waist, gave the signal, and the column once again clanged into action, picking up speed so they could catch up with the spearhead that already had passed from sight. We watched until the last tank passed. Then I turned to my soulmate. "Do you know, my little dove, you could very easily have been killed?"

"I certainly do. That's why I felt it my duty to warn them to be more careful."

"I mean," I started sputtering. "You don't hold up a tank column during maneuvers! It's just not done!"

"It is done. I just did it. There comes a time when a woman must put her foot down." She got on her bike and started up the road, looking at house numbers. "What's the house number we're looking for, dear?"

It was love at first sight when we met Mrs. Ellen Christiansen. Wheeling into the driveway of their attractive suburban home, we had no way of knowing our incessant ringing of her doorbell was interrupting her bath. I was not prepared for the little sprite who came bounding out of the house wearing only a slip and a warm smile of welcome. Before we knew it we were ensconced in a cheery, homey guest room; our bikes were stored in the garage; we had a steaming cup of hot chocolate in our hand; and Mrs. Christiansen had her clothes on.

It is hard to imagine a dynamo in a five-foot package, but the charming little Dane was exactly that. As an artist and a humanitarian, among her many other assets, she showed us some of her landscapes, and told why so many of them depicted swans in the foreground. It seems a previous winter had been severely cold, and the usual habitats of the local swans were frozen over. Knowing the famine that would decimate the swan population, Mrs. Christiansen organized a committee to go out and stomp holes in the ice, and then collect some three thousand dollars for swan food. No small feat in itself—considering there were a hundred different charity drives going on at the same time—convincing people they should part with their kroner to pay for swan food. But collect it she did, and there certainly should be a niche somewhere in the "Nice Folks Hall of Fame" for a genuine, ice-stomping swan saver.

That night, in the town's leading restaurant, we had a delicious dinner consisting of *frikadeller* (Danish meat balls) and pickled beets ($2.00 including a round of beer). Loosening our belts, we decided to take in the local movie. On our way we passed a pastry shop, and checking our good intentions at the door, emerged with three creampuffs that totaled at least ten billion calories.

The theatre was an event in itself. The delightful auditorium was modeled loosely after a Shakespearean theatre; it sold tickets according to tiers, and each ticket was a reserved seat. Buying the best seats in the house (one buck apiece), we settled back to watch the feature—*Mary, Queen of Scots*—which, happily, was in English. I would have enjoyed it more had I not dropped my creampuff on the floor during the first reel, and spent the remainder of the picture wondering how I was going to clean it up. The women enjoyed the film immensely, especially since it brought a feeling of relevancy to the part of the world we were journeying through.

But I, for one, thought the adventures of Mary, Queen of Scots, paled somewhat when compared to Dortha, Queen of the Peugeot, who had single-handedly stopped a tank corps.

Long live Big Red!

7

Bicycle Saddles Can Become Seats of Discontent

THE following morning Mrs. Christiansen insisted we have our breakfast in her greenhouse. Here, surrounded by honey-scented flowers, a grape arbor, four parrots, three canaries, and an emotionally insecure cat that was afraid of birds, we wolfed down an exceptional breakfast of Danish scones, cheeses, eggs, and coffee. And then, to really put the frosting on the cake, the little cherub came lugging out a sack as big as she was, containing a lunch to go. Since her husband worked for the company that makes the mouth-watering *Buko* cheeses, we were the recipients of a repast containing such exotic cheese blends as shrimp, pepper, mushroom, and chocolate.

For two meals and the nicest accommodations we had enjoyed so far on the trip she had the temerity to charge $3.50 per person. Settling up I threw in an extra bill, and was abashed to find the tiny lady shinnying right up my torso to plant a kiss on my cheek.

When we climbed aboard our bikes and prepared to depart, Mrs. Christiansen came running out of the house with a tiny potted plant. "Most bicyclists in Denmark carry a little greenery on their bicycles," she said. "It brings good luck. I want you to have this little coleus, Mrs. Anderson."

Dortha bubbled her thanks, then looked at me. "I love it, Andy, but what'll I do with it? Help me work out something."

"I knew it. Sooner or later it was bound to happen. You had to have an orange tree in your travel trailer. A sprouting sweet-potato vine in your houseboat. I was wondering how long before your green thumb sprouted on your two-wheeled chariot."

Fifteen minutes later the wife had a tiny potted plant wired to the center of her handlebars. "Now you'll have to drive carefully," I said. "No more drag racing or acrobatics."

"I'll do my very best." We all gave Mrs. Christiansen a buss, and shoved off.

We were genuinely sorry to leave.

The weather cooperated beautifully as we struck out for Sakskøbing, our next stop. We soon found ourselves sailing blissfully over the *Storstrømsbroen*, Europe's longest bridge. Complete with bicycle lane, this two-mile miracle of concrete connects Denmark's islands of Sealand and Falster. It was an exciting ride, high over the marine traffic that chugged along the Storstrømmen Strait below. Although a bit of a pull climbing up to its center, we stopped often to enjoy the stimulating view, and then it paid the dividend of a long, free ride down the other side.

The sun warm, a slight breeze on our back, it was sheer enjoyment cycling across the northern tip of Falster. In no time at all we were wheeling over the Guldborgsund that separated the island of Falster from the island of Lolland, the southernmost territory of Denmark.

We stopped at a little fishing village on the sound, bought

some milk from a neighborhood market, and drove out on the wharf to eat the luscious lunch prepared by Ellen Christiansen. We sat there, dangling our feet in the cold, clear water, and throwing crumbs at the fish. A fishing boat pulled in for a load of ice. As if it were the most natural thing in the world, we were soon sitting on the trawler sharing our lunch with the fishermen, who contributed the best smoked herring I've ever eaten, plus half a case of cold Carlsberg "Elephant" beer.

I now know how the beer got its name. Thrown off by its smooth taste, I was unaware of its alcoholic content until I pedaled the length of the wharf before realizing I had forgotten my bicycle. Nevertheless, it was a heartwarming adventure that could only transpire on the back roads, off the tourist track. It's probably the first time the Danish fishermen had ever broken bread with an American family. It was certainly the first time we'd had the good fortune to lunch aboard a Danish fishing boat.

It was a luncheon not to be forgotten. But next time I'm going to forego the elephant beer so I can remember it.

It was early afternoon when we breezed into Sakskøbing. We had no trouble finding accommodations in a small tavern, and, after we had checked our bikes, Dortha and Holly took off in quest of the local laundromat. I went in search of a store that sold sponge rubber.

We were reaching a point in our bicycle conditioning where our muscles were beginning to lose their stiffness. And we could feel our wind gradually building up. But for the old poops, the narrow, hard bike saddle was still a seat of discontent. Although amply endowed by nature with more than our share of rear upholstering, for some reason an irreconcilable incompatibility had developed between seat and sitter. It was my hope to bridge this difference with a thick wedge of foam rubber.

I was successful in my search for a shop that sold sponge rubber. Trying to explain to a very proper, non-English-speaking proprietress why I needed a couple of triangular wedges, however, was another story. Attempting visual communication, I pointed to my fanny, made cycling motions with my legs, and then grimaced. Each time she would look at me oddly over her pince-nez, then point down the block to the local apothecary. Finally, lest I rupture Danish-American relations completely, I measured off a large hunk, paid for it and departed —leaving the nice lady wondering, no doubt, about the peculiar maladies suffered by Americans, whose hemorrhoidal discomfort could be solved only by large slabs of foam rubber.

Back at the hotel I cut the thick material to size, slid the pieces under the bike seat covers, and tested them. They were still by no means a goosedown repository, but they were definitely an improvement. My chore accomplished, and eager to try them out the next morning, I hurried to meet the family at the local laundromat.

We were discovering there are two places in particular where one can always come in contact with European natives. One is in the line waiting to use the hotel bathrooms. The other is in the local laundromat. It was the latter we found the more rewarding, since the people were generally in a better frame of mind.

It was always an experience watching Dortha operate in a foreign washateria. Unlike laundromats at home, which are fairly standardized, the laundries in Europe show rare flashes of originality. No two are alike, due to differences in machine manufacture ranging from Finnish to French. As we were not able to understand the foreign language instructions, it was a fascinating challenge trying to figure out how they worked.

The wife, no slouch when it comes to psychology, had figured a way to beat the system. She entered the establishment affecting the manner of the world's most helpless soul. Human nature being what it is, in no time at all she was surrounded by people eager to help this misbegotten American who was wandering around in a strange land with a bag full of dirty laundry. All she had to do was open her bag, flash her friendly smile, and she had a collection of eager hands coming to her aid.

I entered the laundry to find her as usual—sitting down, flipping through a fashion magazine, and drinking a coke. I looked around to see my unmentionables being washed under the aegis of a cigar-chomping truck driver, being tumbled-dried under the eagle eye of a matronly woman, and being ironed by a pretty young housewife. "How you doing?" I asked, as if I didn't know.

"Soon be ready." She looked up from her magazine long enough to shoot a helpless smile of encouragement at the truck driver. He grinned back, and dumped bleach into my jockey shorts.

"I see you have the situation well in hand."

"Thanks to these marvelous people. I never would have figured this system out. None of the machines take coins." She pointed to a coin box on the wall. "You see, you put a coin in that coin box, and you get a token. Then you put the token into that gizmo over there, and you get a cup of detergent and another token. Then you put the soap and that token into one of the machines." She smiled sweetly at the young housewife who was ironing my shirt. "Isn't that interesting?"

"Fascinating."

Washed, ironed, and neatly folded, our laundry was soon placed in its bag by loving hands. Dortha put down her magazine, made the rounds of the laundromat shaking hands, patting cheeks, bestowing kisses. I picked up the bag, expecting to hear a tearful rendition of *Aloha Oe* as we vacated the premises.

Walking toward the hotel I looked over at the wife. "You fox, you!"

She returned my look, batting her long lashes, the personification of innocence. "I beg your pardon?"

"You fox. Gad, the power of a helpless woman!"

As we would soon be leaving the land of the smorgasbord, we desired to have it one more time before our departure. We were advised by Dortha's old friends at the laundromat that the restaurant in the Hotel Saxkjobing offered the most sumptuous spread in town. We forthwith hied ourselves there for dinner. The advice proved well founded. We soon were up to our wattles in marinated herring, Danish ham, steak and onions, Danish meat roll, liver paste with meat jelly, roast chicken, red cabbage, cucumber salad, cheese, and assorted breads. Topped with peach flambé and coffee, the bill was two dollars per person, everything included.

"Rather than bringing everything in the kitchen out here," said Holly, patting her midriff, "it would be simpler just serving people in the kitchen."

"I never saw so much food in my life," said Dortha.

"These Danes know how to eat," I agreed.

We were also to learn the Danes knew how to drink. Staggering under our load of digestibles, we went to our lodgings. The little tavern was jumping. Not averse to partaking of a small libation on special occasions, I was on the point of joining them for a nightcap. A firm tugging at my ear speedily dictated another course of action, however, and I found myself being engineered up the stairs to our room.

The wife effectively dampered me, but even she could not prevent our room from jumping. We discovered it had been improvidently placed directly above the taproom. It wasn't the singing and laughing and blare of the jukebox (playing old Dean Martin records, yet) that bothered us, as much as the floor stomping and jigging going on downstairs. As we lay in bed watching Dortha's cosmetics waltzing around on the dresser, I said, "Since we seem to be jumping anyway, why don't we go down and join the party?"

"We're going to stay put. Get in shape for a big day tomorrow."

"When in Rome, do as the Rom——"

"We're not in Rome. Go to sleep."

"I was just thinking of the safety standpoint. When the ceiling collapses we'd have an extra floor between us and—"

"Go to sleep."

"Yes, dear."

From this occurrence I added another gem of information to my traveler's lore. When acquiring lodgings at small taverns —and by all means one should—the location of the room should be checked out before signing aboard. If it's over the taproom, unless one is engaged in seismological studies, forget it.

Except if one has an understanding wife, and can join the party.

We arose the next morning hollow-eyed but hungry. Having been warned the tavern served no breakfast, we stumbled into the street in search of sustenance. By sheer happenstance we came across the world's greatest breakfast. In Denmark some of the bakeries have a few tables in the back, where a cup of coffee or tea is served with their pastry. Picking up the scent of freshly baked bread, we followed our noses to a small bakery and went in. As luck would have it, there were tables in the back. We sat down, ordered coffee, and were invited into the baking room to select whatever pastry we desired just as it was popped from the oven.

We were joined by two apple-cheeked moppets belonging to the baker and his wife, who were breakfasting and getting ready for school. One big, happy family, we all sat around supping coffee and partaking of the hot, succulent pastries that kept coming in a never-ending tray from the ovens. It was only when the school bus honked and the moppets bustled off to school—giving us all big bear hugs—that we finally quit gorging ourselves to pursue our own designs.

If I could move that family and pastry shop to Beverly Hills and extract even a minuscule percentage of the profits, I'd make a billion dollars.

Arriving back at the tavern, we were met with a small problem. "The door's locked," said Holly, trying the front door.

"Go on," I said. "Who ever heard of a hotel being locked?" I tried it. It was locked. So was the back door. So were the windows on the ground floor. The place was empty.

"This is ridiculous," said the wife. "How are we going to get our luggage?"

"They're probably closed 'til noon," I said, "when the Danes start drinking their lunch." Poking around, I located a cellar door. I forced it open. Feeling like a gang of cat burglars, we stole through the cellar, up through the kitchen, and climbed an old spiral stairway borrowed from Alfred Hitchcock to our rooms on the second floor. Needless to say, we lost no time in packing, picking up our bikes in the taproom, and spiriting out through the cellar door.

"The bill!" said Dortha, flushed with excitement. "How do we pay the hotel bill?"

"This explains why they wanted payment in advance last night. We're all settled up. Let's get out of here before we're picked up for breaking and entering."

We beat a hasty retreat out of town.

We were sailing along on the back road to Rødbyhavn, where we were to catch the ferry leaving Denmark. The weather was invigoratingly cool but sunny as we churned through the verdant fields and farmlands dotted with whitewashed, flower-bedecked farmhouses. This might have been the reason it dawned on us for the first time. Wheeling into an outdoor café for a midmorning coffee break, it was the wife who put it into words.

"You people know what?"

"What's what," I said, expecting the worst.

"This bicycling. You know, it's downright *fun!*"

I looked at her in surprise. "You're just saying that because your limp's almost gone and you can see out of both eyes again."

"Granted, that's nice. But it just hit me. I'm having a ball!"

"Maybe it's the foam rubber I put in your bicycle seat. You're floating on air."

"Hardly. My sitter's still sore. Instead of being sore in one spot, you've managed to spread it around to a larger area. But in spite of that—my bruises, my black eye—I just realized it for the first time. This is absolutely great."

"Well!" I said, beaming. I looked over at my daughter. "And what do you think, Holly?"

"I've loved every minute, Dad. You know that."

"Not just because you'd be back in school if you weren't here?"

"Not at all. This is ten times the education I'd be getting in a school quarter. This is the bee's knees, Pop."

"Then I have a confession to make," I said. "I haven't had so much fun since we went down the Mississippi in the houseboat."

And it was true. Maybe because we were getting conditioned to the bicycles. Maybe because of the adventure of new places, meeting great people. Maybe because it was such a completely different, unregimented do-your-own-thing, not-knowing-where-you're-going-to-spend-the-night freedom that people spend so much time looking for and seldom find. Whatever it was, it was marvelous. And I was overjoyed to find the rest of the family was enjoying it as much as I.

It was fortunate that everyone was in such a good mood. For shortly before lunch we came upon a condition that put it sorely to the test. The farmers were burning their fields, preparatory to new planting. At one point, near the road, a landowner was tending a fire that was sending up great billows of gray smoke. We waved gaily as we spun by; he returned our wave with a big smile.

And then a capricious wind did us dirt. We were suddenly enveloped by a great cloud of choking, dense smoke that cut visibility to absolute zero. Being in the lead, I stopped and tried to turn around to warn the followers. Blinded by the smoke I managed to stop, but became completely disoriented. I heard, rather than saw, Holly whiz by me coming in the opposite direction. And then Dortha, from a completely different direction.

For what seemed like hours the three of us milled around in the gagging gray, barely missing one another. At one point we were playing dodge'm with a Volkswagen that was having the same problem. In addition to upsetting the orientational senses, the smoke was hot and asphyxiating. I was beginning to get genuinely worried about my troops.

Then, as quickly as it had come upon us, the breeze shifted. Bright sunlight exposed a scene reminiscent of an Ethiopian fire drill. Dortha was energetically trying to climb a steep bank on the far side of the road. Holly was mired in a ditch on the opposite side. I was on a collision course with a large cow that was even more confused than I.

Exhaling smoke and wiping tears from our eyes, we speedily vacated the scene. Down the road we stopped to take a head count and beat the smoke from our clothes. The VW we had skirmished with in the blackout came charging up the road, dragging a long plume of smoke. "I thought that VW was heading in the other direction," I said, happy to find my voice box still functioning.

"I thought so, too," said Dortha. "One of us is going the wrong way."

I checked the sun. At least we were heading in the right direction. "Everybody all right?"

"Where does it say," said Dortha, removing her head scarf and releasing a puff of smoke, "that nice redhead has to turn into smoked ham on crazy man's bicycle trip?"

I looked at the smudgy, tear-streaked faces of my flock and started chuckling.

"Crazy man has weird sense of humor," said Holly, blowing her nose.

"May we hear one more time," I said, "how much you all are enjoying your bicycle trip?"

It was lunchtime, and it looked like an ideal place for a picnic, right by the side of the road. A carpet of lush grass extended in all directions. I gave the signal and whipped the wagons into a circle.

The women dismounted and began their culinary preparations that never ceased to amaze me. How a cornucopic repast could issue from tiny bicycle saddlebags was a feat of ingenuity I ranked just ahead of the moonshot. First, the plastic tablecloth came from Dortha's bag, followed by cheese and lunch meat. From Holly's panniers came bread spread with butter, plastic glasses, and juice-squirting pears and clusters of fat grapes. Not to be outdone, I produced a bottle of good wine picked up at a grocery store a few clicks back. "Where's the candelabra?" I said, sitting down before the elegant picnic spread.

"Oh, you want candles?" asked Holly, making motions toward her bike.

"I'm kidding already. Let's eat."

We did. Whatever else may be argued about the therapeutic benefits of cycling, there is one point that bears repeating. It takes lots of fuel. After a full morning in the saddle, there's precious little time lost between dish and dentures. Cold lunch meat tastes like beef Wellington, cold cheese like lobster New-burg, a cooky like baked Alaska.

We were just salivating through our cheese and fruit dessert when I noticed something skimming toward me across the lawn. A large object plopped into my lap. I looked down. "I didn't ask anyone to pass the soccer ball."

"No one passed the soccer ball," said the wife.

"Then why is there one in my lap?" I looked to one end of the field. I was chagrined to see we were no longer alone in our idyllic setting. We had been invaded. I beheld a dozen young men wearing red jerseys and bruised kneecaps. At the other end of the field were a dozen young men wearing blue jerseys and bruised kneecaps. We were situated precisely between them. Another soccer ball whizzed by, upsetting the wine bottle. "Well, whaddaya know," I said, looking sheepishly at my kin.

"I know," said Dortha, scurrying to her feet. "The old wagon master has done it again. You picked a great place to have a picnic. In the middle of a soccer field."

"I was wondering about all those bleachers. Which team you betting on? Blue jerseys or red?"

"I'm betting we better get out of here. Like right now."

"You may have a point."

Just as we were leaving the field I heard Holly shout, "*Hey, Peugeots!*" Looking around I saw two young men cycling down the bike trail in the classical pelvis-to-the-sky configuration that marks the dedicated cycling tourist. Hearing the yell, especially delivered by a female voice, there was the squeal of rubber. The lads spun around and approached. They were the first touring cyclists we had seen since starting the trip, and they, too, were riding Peugeots.

"You speak English," said the taller of the two, a good-looking, well-proportioned young man.

"Not very well," said Holly. "We're Americans."

"Capital!" said the short one. I noticed a large bandage on his left knee. "We're Canadians."

"Put 'er there," said Holly, putting it there.

It turned out the two young men were on their way to Copenhagen, having started from England. They were staying at youth hostels en route and doing some sort of research paper for their college theses. They were loaded down even more than we, carrying a tent, cooking utensils, and bedrolls. "Would you join us in a cup of tea?" asked the short one.

"Delighted," said Holly, assuming command. "Let's go over to the bleachers where we can sit down."

"Capital. We'll gather around and watch the pot boil."

Staking out nice bleacher seats we got comfortable while the young men prepared tea. The short one reached into his pannier and produced a small aluminum gadget slightly larger than a deck of cards, and unfolded a tiny camp stove. As he screwed a small can of butane into it and lit it, his partner produced a folding aluminum pot, filled it with water from a canteen, and placed it on the stove. "Tea water will soon be hot," he said.

"That's quite a contraption," I said. "Has to be the world's smallest stove. Work good?"

"Works great. Made in Sweden. Oh-oh—I just happened to remember. We're missing one ingredient for our tea."

"A tea bag," said the wife.

He snapped his fingers. "That's it. I think we used the last one this morning."

"Just happen to have some," said the wife. "You prefer jasmine or orange pekoe?" She rummaged around in her purse. "I'm afraid they're the only two choices. The Chinese tea seems to be all gone."

I looked at my wife in awe. "Since when did you start carrying tea bags in your purse?"

"Since I found there wasn't room for my samovar." She handed several tea bags to the young man. "Anyone care for cream or sugar?"

As we drank our tea the ingratiating young bucks regaled us with their cycling adventures thus far. In spite of a few problems, the trip was blossoming into a glorious adventure. Not being experienced cyclists before they started, they, too, had picked up their share of various and sundry bruises. Not the least of which had been contributed by a sneaky tree limb. The bandaged knee on the shorter Canadian had been the result of a trip through Holland when he made the mistake of rising up on his seat at precisely the same spot an overhanging branch canopied the bike trail. He was literally speechless to find himself hanging by his larynx, while his riderless bike continued serenely down the road. When he flopped to the ground he was dismayed to find his kneecap was facing the opposite direction he was. A local medic helped overcome this small dilemma and, bloody but unbowed, they proceeded on their way.

There are worse ways to while away an hour than drinking tea and watching a Danish soccer game in the company of two gregarious Canadian cyclists. Even though I did contribute two kroner to the Maple-leafers by betting on the blue jerseys. When we parted company we all regretted we were not going in the same direction.

Particularly Holly.

We rolled through the bustling city of Rødbyhavn, and were directed to the ferry terminal by courteous natives. It was here we would debark for Germany.

At the Danish customs office at the terminal, I dismounted and went in. There had been speculation on the part of Mr. Norit, our ebullient bike salesman, that the "moms" tax we had paid on our bicycles might be refunded if we could prove we were exporting them out of the country. Since we were riding the bikes out under the very noses of the customs people, and since the tax amounted to some sixty dollars, I thought it worth a try.

Explaining my mission, I was ushered into the office of the ranking customs man, a gargantuan Dane with an infectious smile and a bubbling sense of humor. His joviality bubbled right into a mirthful boil when I informed him of the purpose of my visit.

"So you thought you were going to get some tax money back," he said, between gleeful bellows.

"I had been led to believe so, yes, sir."

Caught up anew in the hilarity of the situation, he addressed the gathering customs officials. "This gentleman thinks he's going to get some tax money back. Did you fellows hear that?"

The fellows heard it, and joined in the merriment.

"My good man," he said, clapping my shoulder and wrapping me in the warmth of his smile. "That's why I love you Americans. Great sense of humor. Of course you know we Danes never let any money out of the country. We just take it in." This was the signal for another round of hearty guffaws.

"That's sorta the way I had it pegged," I said, joining in with a hollow chuckle.

"Awful nice of you to drop by." He wiped tears of mirth from his cheeks. "Anytime you're by this way. What a sense of humor!"

"Thank you, sir. Glad I was able to add a little sunshine to your day." His booming laugh propelled me right through the customs door.

"How did you make out?" asked the wife, waiting outside with the bikes.

"I found out I have a great sense of humor."

"That's all?"

"I also found out we have been legally divorced from sixty bucks. There is one bright note, however."

"What's that?"

"We have visitation rights. We can come to Denmark any time and see our money."

"How nice."

We stopped at the handy little bus that served as a rolling currency converter, and changed all our Danish money to German. Then, luck being with us, we rolled right onto a ferry just preparing to depart.

Although conditioned by the excellent Scandinavian service that plows the sound between Norway and Sweden, we still were not prepared for the beautiful German ferryboat that would lift us from Denmark to Deutschland. The previous crossing had been on the train ferry at night, and we had not ventured from our railroad car parked in the bowels of the boat. This return trip was the first time we had really seen the big ship.

Our bikes were quickly secured by eager young stevedores. (Having Holly along was an asset in more ways than one.) We took an elevator up to the promenade and walked through pneumatic doors that sprang open at the touch of a button. Parting company momentarily to use the immaculate rest rooms, we rejoined in the elegant dining salon that made Maxim's of Paris look like McDonald's of Perth Amboy.

We toured the duty-free shops where Dortha picked up a bottle of perfume and Holly acquired a huge box of marzipan candy. Unable to resist the three-dollar price of a quart of Cutty Sark, I bought it and a carton of Benson & Hedges—even if it meant cycling with them on my head. Then Holly and I decided to go up on deck to watch the departure.

Father and daughter stood at the rail, watching the huge

ferry backing slowly from its slip. A light fog was moving in, shrouding the harbor in eerie wisps of gray. "I really hate to leave Denmark," said Holly, putting her arm through mine. "It's *so* lovely."

"One of my favorite countries in all the world," I said. "Even though the customs officials have a weird sense of humor."

"I want to come back some day. Wouldn't it be a marvelous place to teach?"

"That it would."

Silently we watched the boat turn, then head out through the harbor, emitting deep growls of warning from its thunderous horns. The fog thickened fast, the shoreline of Denmark was quickly out of sight. Its course now charted by radar, the big ship groped its way through the swirling, misty twilight zone toward the coast of Germany.

8

"A Cowpie a Threat to Navigation? Ridic——!"

I had been unable to get any information about a good bike route that led through northern Germany to the Netherlands. Available maps showed autobahns and arterial roads that veined this part of the country, but I had no desire to risk life, limb, or Cutty Sark bottle on these no-speed-limit corridors of collision. And we had been warned that even the better cycling routes sometimes had poor road surfaces and long stretches of cobbled roads and tram tracks that dictated the use of heavy-duty wheels and tires.

Consequently, we decided to take the train from Putt-garden—where our ferry docked on the north German coast—and proceed west to the easternmost part of Holland. It was the Low countries that appealed to us—where cars, not bicycles, were the minority. The Netherlands, Belgium, northern France—these countries were paradise to the pedaler.

Pulling into the fogbound ferry terminal at Puttgarden, we went directly to the train station to procure tickets for Groningen, Holland. Blessed with an English-speaking ticket clerk, we checked our bikes through (costing only fifty cents apiece with passenger tickets), and found *beforehand* we would have to change trains at Hamburg. Since there would be a long layover in Hamburg in the wee small hours, we decided to spend the night there and proceed on to Groningen the next day, where our bikes would be waiting. Hopefully.

The two-hour ride to Hamburg was pleasant, but the city itself was miserable. Spoiled by the tranquility of small towns and villages, it was a shock to be disgorged into a big, teeming, dirty city. Checking in at the information booth at the station, we found a hotel near the depot, had a bite to eat at a Chinese restaurant, and turned in early after a long day. I wasn't even too disappointed when Dortha vetoed my plan to cruise through Hamburg's world-famous red-light district—the city's main claim to fame.

We were eager to get out of the city the next morning, and it was an interesting train trip through northern Germany, in spite of a heavy rain. We were glad to see the drooling skies get it out of their system so we would have fair weather when we picked up our bicycles. As we crossed the border it was almost possible to see the line of demarcation that separated the Netherlands from Germany. The green fields of Holland came into view, manicured as neatly as the front lawns and flowers that surrounded the pin-neat farmhouses.

Pulling into the station at Groningen, we went immediately to the baggage room to redeem our bicycles. They had not arrived. As best we could tell from the baggage clerk, whose command of English was on a par with my command of Dutch, the cycles might arrive sometime during the day. Rather than moon over the delay, we decided to see the city.

The tourist bureau being in the center of town and too far to walk to, we hailed a taxi. We had no way of knowing we had picked a cab being driven by Evel Knievel until we roared off toward the downtown section. It was bedlam! It was also noon, which seemed to be the signal for everyone to jump on his bicycle and go someplace. Never had we seen so many bikes. Nor so many people from different walks of life riding two-wheelers. Businessmen, secretaries, flower peddlers, milkmen, mailmen, even policemen pumped through the city, completely oblivious to any four-wheeled vehicle that had the temerity to intrude.

The cab driver, evidently used to being hopelessly outnumbered, solved his insecurities by the simple expedient of leaning heavily on his horn and accelerator. Like a cruiser breasting a heavy chop, he bluffed his way through the sea of cycling bodies. How we ever reached the square without bagging at least one unbluffable biker is something I'll never understand. Needless to say, it was with supreme relief that we finally alighted and discharged our cabbie.

Groningen is a lovely city, carpeted with parks and greenery and wall-to-wall flowers. The tourist bureau quickly had us reservations in a pension, and anxious to divest ourselves of our luggage, we again flagged down a cab to take us to the address. Of all the cabs in the city, we found we had again enlisted the services of Evel Knievel. Before we could back out, we were shooting the rapids through the white water of handlebars, bike baskets, and tail reflectors with the throttle firewalled.

Vowing never again to rent a taxi in Holland, we weathered the wild ride to shakily dismount on a narrow side street. Happily, it was clean and devoid of dog doo, for the three of us spent considerable time kissing the ground.

A matronly woman with bulging brisket and butter cheeks met us at the door of the pension. We soon found why the room was so inexpensive. It was on the top of five floors! The only way of egress was a circular stairway resembling a fireman's pole nicked with steps. When we finally reached the summit with our baggage, I fought the urge to plant a flag.

"Good grief," whispered Dortha. "I'll bet a buck Neil Simon lives here."

"If he does," I panted, "I'm sure he's married to an oxygen bottle."

The puffing proprietress showed us to our room and unlocked the door. The three of us staggered to the first bed, then collapsed on it. Simultaneously. Not to be outdone, the bed collapsed. This unfortunate incident proved as embarrassing to the landlady as to us. While I apologized for my family throwing such an unaccustomed load on one defenseless bed, she apologized for having a bed with such an inferior foundation. By the time we scrounged new slats and reassembled the four-poster, we and the proprietress had become old friends. She and Dortha exchanged addresses, and I'm sure we'll be exchanging Christmas cards for years to come.

That afternoon we took a walking tour of the pretty, canal-veined city. Dortha and Holly scouted the nice stores while I watched the canal boats and marine traffic bearing flags of all nations cruising the damp boulevards. In the course of my travels I came across a fine pub where the delicious Dutch Heineken beer was dispensed over tables made from old beer kegs. I collected my troops and took them to the tavern. Here we had a lively happy-hour mingling with the delightful Dutch as they dissolved their workday tensions in the bubbles of malt and grape.

Hankering to dine at a typical Holland restaurant, we found one near the city square, and came laboring out under a load of delicious meat croquettes and Dutch pancakes—wondering how we would ever get them up the five flights to our room.

Then, too stuffed to do anything else, we succumbed to the enticements of a downtown theatre's marquee. Intrigued by the idea of hearing Barbra Streisand singing in Dutch, we caught the first show. Barbra sang in English with Dutch subtitles, but it didn't matter, as we had more fun watching the Hollanders rolling in the aisles over the farcical romp of sight gags that comprised *What's Up, Doc?* The most redeeming part of the whole evening was the Dutch theatre that provided a mezzanine where one could retire for a cup of coffee whenever the movie lagged.

I ended up giving the picture a five-cup rating.

The next morning we were pleasantly surprised to find there was none of this continental breakfast nonsense for the Dutch. It was little wonder our puffing proprietress complained of chest pains, for she came struggling up to the summit of Mount McKinley with a breakfast as big as she was. We broke fast in bed, yet. Delicious ham, eggs, cheese, breads, and jams disappeared like dew before the morning sun.

After breakfast we bade a sorrowful good-bye to our landlady, then walked to the station, hoping our bikes would be there. They were. Anxious to dive into the swim of bicycles, we saddled up swiftly and were on our way, heading for the wide open spaces.

On my sojourn through Groningen the previous afternoon I had tracked down a bookstore that carried maps, hoping to find one depicting cycling roads through Holland. My search was rewarded by a rare find: a map designed specifically for cycles and small motorbikes. It delineated the best bike roads, as well as routes through large cities. It also showed the freeways and busy arterials that were closed to cycles—with alternate routes, in this case, that enabled the pedaler to chart his own course with a minimum of frustration.

And it showed, oh, happy day, roads that were exclusively for bikes, closed to four-wheeled vehicles. Even the design of the map was addressed to the two-wheeler. Instead of being one big page, like our American maps which, once unfolded, positively defied efforts to refold it the same way; this map was cut into strips, each strip folding out like a dress pleat. This allowed it to be opened at any point, then tucked under the plastic map case on the handlebar bag used by many cycling tourists. For our purpose it was heaven-sent.

Following our map we whisked through traffic, having only one near miss with a taxi driver I recognized as our Evel Knievel. Not only were the bike routes well marked through the outskirts of town, but in the busier sections there were actually bicycle freeways—complete with speed lanes! And for the first time we saw signal lights on the cycle paths. Miniature traffic signals with bicycle silhouettes on the red, green, and amber lights. At last we were really in honest-to-God bike country. As Holly said, truly a cyclepathic experience.

Quickly shunted through the city's outskirts, we passed into a panoramic pastoral setting that had been scrubbed clean and green by the departing rains. We rolled through farmland supporting the finest livestock we had ever seen. Occasional windmills, blades rotating slowly in a freshening breeze, lapped up water from the canals to spread over pastured land. If one desired to make postcard pictorials depicting cycle touring at its most photogenic, this was the place.

We rotated along, Dortha emitting squeals of delight over the calendar-picture cottages, the fields of flowers, the picturesque natives—some still clomping around in wooden shoes. And the bicycles! Right out of the pages of *National Geographic* rode a pipe-smoking Dutchman delivering milk from huge cans strapped to his cycle; a buxom matron spoking along a load of golden-wheeled cheese that would have sprung the axles of a Mack truck; a young girl dressed in a rainbow costume complete with lace hat, stroking toward class with a violin case under her arm.

We slowed to thread through a herd of goats being driven

by the scuff-scuff of an oldtimer's wooden shoes extending beyond the pedals of his bicycle. "Now, this is living," said Dortha. "This morning alone makes the trip worthwhile. I'd just like to fold up this whole countryside and take it back to California."

"No way," said Holly, the environmentalist. "In twenty-four hours we'd have three freeways running through it, the flowers smogged to death, and the canals full of Dixie cups and beer cans. Let's leave it right where it is."

Hypoxic with the weather, the beauty of the surroundings, the great cycling roads, we were feeling a little kittenish. Holly and I were acting up, performing acrobatics on our bikes. She was swinging along, riding with no hands, pretending she was reading a book. Not to be outdone, I took my hands off the grips, leaned back on my bike and pretended to take a nap. "Look, ma, no hands," I said, sailing by Dortha in a supine position while giving vent to several rattling snores.

"Look out!" she said. "Up ahead."

I saw it, but too late. My front wheel hit it right smack in the middle, then started sliding in the slippery mess. Before I could grab the handlebars I was in the ditch grabbing water lilies. Protected from injury by the marshy bank, I picked myself up to confront my distaff. I tried to camouflage my embarrassment with a spiritless chuckle.

"Look, ma," she said. "No teeth. You trying to get yourself killed, you big clown?"

"I saw it," I said, wiping mud from my pants.

"Then why did you run over it?"

"Just testing. I've done a lot of traveling, but this is the first conveyance I've ever used where a cowpie can be a threat to navigation."

We stopped for lunch by a huge, creaking windmill. Holly brought out sandwiches made from breakfast leftovers, and I uncorked a bottle of milk picked up at a little store. Dortha made a centerpiece of wild flowers picked nearby, and, famished as always, we lit into the luncheon.

"*Gllurrrack!*" said Dortha, taking a swallow of milk. She looked at me. "Why, husband? Tell me why."

"Why what?"

"Why in the middle of the world's richest dairyland do you have to buy powdered milk?"

I looked at the plastic milk bottle. Sure enough, it was rejuvenated powdered milk. "Sorry about that. From now on I'll get wine. Not too much powdered wine around."

Grudges are not compatible with full stomachs, and I was eventually forgiven as we all lay down in the warm sun for a short snooze before hitting the trail again.

Sometime later, steering through a gaggle of geese, Dortha said, "Where are we going to spend the night, love?"

I honked back at a big honker that was honking at me. "I haven't the foggiest idea. Why?"

"I dunno. Just curious." She laughed. "Isn't this something? Me, a dame who feeds on an orderly, well-disciplined routine, pedaling through a herd of honkers somewhere in Holland, not having the remotest idea where my next pillow's coming from? And what's more, not caring in the least? How does that grab you?"

"Great. Just great. You always worry too much."

"Maybe I'm beginning to see the light. Or maybe it's just this beautiful, tranquil scenery."

"A contribution, no doubt. But I think we're beginning to get infected with this spoked-wheel mania. I knew there had to be more to bike touring than just the jollies of rupturing your spleen on a leather buffalo horn. It's another world. Poking along at our own pace, pausing to snoop, snooze, or satisfy the inner man whenever we feel like it—I gotta confess I'm getting hooked."

"Well, before we get completely carried away, mayhap we should be thinking about a place to bed down pretty soon."

"There are lots of little villages along this road to Leeuwarden. When you get tired, I'm sure we can find room at an inn. If not"—I motioned toward a nearby barn—"mayhap you and I could shack up in a cozy barn loft? Play a little nice-nice in the hay?"

"You and your hay fetish. Forget it, Charley."

"Spoilsport."

It was fortunate we were on a very loose schedule this day. Around midafternoon we came to a detour on the bicycle path. The road was torn up with the installation of new paving. We followed the detour sign up a sleepy side road and eventually became completely lost. This was not disagreeable, as our road followed a sparkling stream that moseyed through a stretch of woods tunneling the lane with its branches. We had no idea where we would end up, but it had to be a nice place.

And it was. Our first clue was a warning road sign, visually depicting an elderly lady with a cane. A caution to motorists. In a short time we were upon the reason for the warning. A row of low buildings, very attractive and beautifully landscaped, were strung around a shimmering blue lake. Around the lake's dancing fountain swam swans and wild ducks. It was, without doubt, the most beautiful home for the elderly we had ever seen.

Here, age had added another wheel to the precarious bicycle. Three-wheelers roamed the premises. Some substituting for wheelchairs. Young ladies in crisp blue uniforms were in attendance, cheerfully catering to the needs of the elderly. One was supervising a three-wheeled bicycle race in progress. Two ancient gladiators, whose flesh may have flagged but whose spirits had not, were whipping their chariots around the baby duck pond where we stood watching. Dortha became the object of a gummy grin from the leading contestant, who almost ended up in the duck pond for his flirtation.

"Isn't this marvelous?" said Dortha. "Look at the way these old folks are treated with love and veneration."

"And this is some comfortable nest," I said. "A person could age with dignity in a place like this."

"Just look at those happy faces. Why can't we tear a page from Holland's handbook on treatment of the elderly? In our country as soon as they reach the age where they're no longer a viable consumer for television marketing, they might as well shove out to sea like the old Eskimos."

"If they weren't such a handy source of revenue for our muggers, our oldsters would probably be banned from society altogether."

We would have loved a tour of the premises. To be briefed on the whole structure of the socialized program for senior citizens in the Netherlands. But the shadows were lengthening, and it was time to find a trundle bed for the night. So we got directions from one of the pleasant nurses and headed off toward the nearest hotel.

It was just a fork in the road, but the rooms in the little hotel were clean, and the owner most congenial. In the hotel dining room he personally officiated to whomp up a tantalizing dinner of chicken curry, and in the process we met his two precocious children and his pretty wife. He spoke excellent English, having served as chief steward on a Shell Oil tanker, and her English was almost as good, being from New York's Bronx.

There is something about spending a day on the fendered exerciser, however, that tends to hang tiny sandbags on the eyelids at a very early hour. Even stimulating conversation and a double brandy with coffee did not stem the lids in their downward flight. There was nothing to do but drag ourselves up to the comforters and knuckle under to the god Morpheus.

We were up with the roosters the next morning, and out on the trail in weather too good to be true. The validity of that weather statement hit us after biking through the colorful city of Leeuwarden. Just on the other side of town the weather was, indeed, too good to be true. It became so bad it was unbelievable.

Not particularly nasty in a climatological sense. No monsoons, typhoons, or tidal waves; but for a bicycle rider it could have been more frustrating only in the degree of intensity. It was a 25-knot wind gusting head-on into the handlebars. For the first time we really found out how wind can affect progress on a bike. It was as if we'd turned a corner at Leeuwarden, and blam! Right into an invisible brick wall. In the lead, I was tooting along grandly one minute, the next I was toppling over on my bike, not creating enough momentum to stay erect.

This demanded a strategy meeting. I honked for a huddle behind an old barn. The team gathered around. "Okay, gang. We seem to be hitting some opposition. But we're gonna win. We're gonna plow right through the cold front. Sort of a reverse-modified Statue of Liberty play."

"Gotcha," said Holly. "Old number seventeen. Never fails."

"Right. Now, I'll run interference. Block the wind. Big Red, you right behind me. Up close to my tail to take advantage of the interference. Holly, you next. Right behind Big Red. Okay, team. Any questions?"

"One," said Holly. "Isn't it about lunchtime?"

"We'll eat down the road a few clicks. Little town called Franeker. Now, we'll have to treat the wind like a steep grade. Shift down 'til you can pedal comfortably. Tuck in as close behind me as you can." I slapped them both on the rump. "Get in there, team, and fight."

"I have to go to the bathroom," said Big Red.

We gave it a college try. Hunched down as far as we could to cut down wind resistance, we looked like a single file of

Quasimodos. We downshifted through ten speeds, would have gone to an alpine gear if we had one. Our feet rotated like butter churners, only to have this energy translated into inches gained on the ground. Barely able to maintain equilibrium, we clawed and scratched for every meter. We found that no mode of transportation allows a closer study of the terrain over which one is passing than biking into a high wind. At one point, bent to the horizontal, my eyes on the road directly in front of me, I watched a large ant scurrying along, making better time than I was. And he was dragging a big beetle.

We looked forward to every house, tree, passing truck —anything that afforded a momentary windbreak. For a brief instant the giant hand would quit pushing against us, and we'd all but fall forward on our faces during a momentary spurt. Then, wham! We'd be stopped in our tracks. We cut our rest breaks from every half hour to every quarter hour. Finally, during a climaxing gust that froze us stationary, we dismounted and pushed our bikes into the blast. "I wasn't kidding," said the wife, the wind tearing the words from her lips.

"About what?" I said.

"About having to go to the bathroom."

"You pick the most uncanny times to have to—"

"That's my problem. I don't see any around."

I looked. There was one scraggly tree nearby, its leaves being whipped by the wind. "Over yonder is a—"

"No way," she said, following my eyes. "I'm not exposing my bloomers to this gale. I'd be kited right into France."

I checked my fluttering map. "There's a village up the road about a kilometer. Can you make it?"

"Faced with no alternative, I'll make it. But I guarantee it'll be the longest kilometer on record."

"I could hail down a car."

"I'll make it."

"You got great grit, girl."

It turned out to be a kilometer, all right, but a click that was 150 miles long. Nothing can provide quite the stimulus of kinetic kidneys, however, and the last hundred meters the good wife's pumping pedals were a blur of motion. We wheeled into the first gas station. Dortha was in the restroom before her bike wheels stopped turning.

Much to everyone's relief, including the gas station attendant's.

Except for such emergencies, we generally availed ourselves of restroom facilities at the little cafés or taverns where we stopped for frequent coffee breaks. This was expected, and the accommodations were generally quite comfortable. On the rare occasions when forced to use gas station W.C.s, we found them almost as interesting as European taverns. Especially those off the beaten path.

In the States I was equipped with nearly the complete gamut of gasoline credit cards. And with a thirsty Buick that homes in on gas stations like a mongrel mutt to fireplugs, we were always welcomed with open arms. As a cyclist, however, I at first feared the reception we would get when approaching a gas station. The restroom facilities were going to be utilized, and the only prospect for service payment would be an occasional shot of free air in a bicycle tire, or perhaps a spurt of water for Dortha's plant. An arrangement hardly calculated to send a station manager into soaring flights of financial extravagance.

My fears proved unfounded after several visits to European petrol ports. Not wishing to be a cheapskate, I'd sometimes purchase a road map in return for their courtesy, blowing as much as a quarter. But even this proved unnecessary. Most rural Europeans are still more obsessed with the race of man than with the race of the rat, and could care less whether you bought anything. Just the chance to chat with a stranger, particularly a foreigner, was more than adequate compensation for towels and tissues a visitor used in the washroom.

And on the subject of continental toilet tissue, a book could be written on this item alone. Especially that found in rural service stations. It runs the spectrum from crushed corn-stalks to a brittle, nonabsorbent sheet that could only be manu-factured by Alcoa. Probably a good ecological investment, since it's undoubtedly reusable. Dortha had licked the problem on her first day of biking by carrying her own. Not for any particular hygienic reason, but, as she put it, "After a day on that bicycle I refuse to add insult to parts already injured."

While Holly and Dortha were in the rest room, the station attendant admired our bikes, I admired his station, and then we launched into an interesting sign-language cracker-barrel discussion about the price of cheese, the economy of Holland, Florida's new Disneyland, and why Dutch damsels don't wear hot pants. When the women finally emerged, Dortha wearing a broad smile indicating a much gladder bladder, we bade a grateful adieu and thrust out again into the wind.

It took us all morning to make ten miles. When we finally blew into Franeker, we were famished and fatigued. Locating a little park in the center of town, we expired on the inviting grass that surrounded a small lake. Sandwiches were produced and devoured before they had a chance to hit the tablecloth. Huddled down behind a small dune, spitting blowing sand from our bread, we realized we were not the only ones taking ad-vantage of the lake.

It seemed to be some sort of weird ritual signaled by the twelve o'clock gong of the town church. All types of people suddenly materialized around the little body of water: clerks, la-borers, school kids, the town constable. Nearly all were car-rying a folding chair slung over their shoulder, most toting a sun umbrella in addition. The chairs were carefully unfolded, bodies installed, then protected from the elements by raised umbrellas. Once comfortable, fishing poles were produced, snapped together, worms introduced to hooks, and lines dropped into the water. This chore completed, hands were dipped into lunch sacks.

We watched the performance in astonishment. The lunch-time anglers blissfully munched their lunches and watched their bobbing corks, completely oblivious to the wind snapping their umbrellas—at times threatening to upend them, chair and all, into the lake. In my experience with the wet world, I have done my share of fishing, have witnessed many aficionados of Izaak Walton. Never in my life, however, had I seen angling being done in quite such comfort or with such studied indifference.

There surely must have been something in the lake. Some kind of finned panfish that beckoned this interesting array of worm drowners. But if there was, they were either off their feed or couldn't see the bait because of the whipping waves. In any event, we never saw so much as one cork bobble, let alone a fish get beached.

Dortha and Holly soon bored of the excitement, pulled the tablecloth over them as protection from the wind, and dropped off to sleep. I was too interested in the fishermen to join them, and watched in vain for the first cork to go under. Then the church gong sounded one o'clock. This was the signal for everyone to reel in his hook, disassemble his pole, fold up his chair and umbrella, and quietly disappear to pursue appointed duties in other quarters. Five minutes later there was not a soul to be seen.

Wondering if maybe I, too, hadn't fallen asleep and dreamed this whole eerie happening, I roused the crew and headed down the road.

It was our desire to make Harlingen before nightfall, as

this was reputed to be one of the most picturesque old fishing villages in Holland, and a sight worth seeing. It was only ten miles to the west, and we all swore to make it, come hell or high water. As it turned out, the high water came first, and then the hell. Halfway to our destination—and miles from nowhere—it started to rain.

And it didn't rain in drops. Somebody pulled the plug in the heavens.

9

Zinging over the Zuider Zee

FEELING the first drops, I honked for a conference. We gathered under a bridge. "We've still got about eight clicks to go," I said. "It's been tough enough riding smack into the face of this wind. It's gonna be twice as tough with the wind full of wet teeth. Anyone want to abort this mission and find a farmhouse stable?"

"You said there was a good seafood restaurant in Harlingen," said Holly. "I'm for going on."

"So noted." I looked at Dortha. "And you, First Mate?"

She looked around her, trying to pierce the scudding mist. "I don't see a farmhouse for miles around. Let alone a stable. And even though this bridge has running water, it's not my idea of a great place to spend the night. I don't think we have a heckuva lotta choice, Skipper. Let's keep going."

"So be it. Damn the torpedos."

At first it was just uncomfortable. The slashing rain stung our faces, found ingress through the openings in our ponchos. The wind was an immovable object against our indomitable

138

force. I plowed through in the lead, breaking the wind, the others nose to tail behind me. In our windbreakers we resembled a giant yellow caterpillar inching along the road. The Battle for Pork Chop Hill paled beside the energy expended in gaining an inch of ground.

Four clicks to go. A click, or kilometer, is five-eighths of a mile. It is not a terribly long distance. On a bicycle in a driving rain, however, spending nearly as much time going backward as forward, one kilometer is the distance to the moon.

Three clicks to go. The heavens decided to quit piddling around with the sprinkles and settle down to some serious raining. Exerting all our energy to take advantage of a windbreak offered by a row of trees bordering the road, we didn't see it coming. A truck came by, hit a small lagoon near the bike trail, and splashed its contents over the three of us. Momentarily blinded, we stopped under the nearest tree. "Well, troops," I said, wiping muddy water out of my eyes, "according to my odometer we have three clicks to go. Everybody having a good time?"

Holly looked at me in stony silence. The wife tilted her head up to look at me from under the brim of her rain hat. This sent a small puddle of water cascading down the back of her neck. Shivering, she said, "I think I'll bite your head."

"That's my love." I wiped away a little stream that was waterfalling off the end of her nose. "That's the fighting spirit that carries us through these little problems."

"Little problems! The Holland dike just broke, and you call it a little problem."

Two clicks to go. The transition from discomfort to misery had long since passed. I was getting concerned. And then something happened to add to my consternation. The asphalt road of the bike trail suddenly switched to cobblestones. Being in the lead, I was the first to discover there are few things slicker than wet cobblestones. One second I was riding my bike, the next second it was riding me. The others, seeing me spread-eagled under my Peugeot, stopped before they, too, were up-ended by the slippery surface.

"Are you hurt, honey?"

I looked up at the dripping face of my wife. "No. Just thought I'd rest a minute."

She plunked down beside me. "Thank God."

"I'm getting worried about you and Holly, though. We've got over a mile to go. And we won't be able to ride on these cobblestones. I'm going to hail down a ride for you two."

"Don't be silly. In the first place, a car hasn't gone by since that truck that tried to drown us. In the second place, we're not about to leave our wagon master."

"I know you two are bone tired. I should have stopped for the night in Franeker. I'm real sorry I got you into this—"

I felt a cold forefinger on my lips. "Hush. We're doing fine. In another hour we'll be in a hot shower laughing about all this." She helped me to my feet.

"You know, Red, you're a confusing female. The more gritchy and overcast a situation becomes, the sunnier your disposition gets. You're all mixed up."

She flashed her teeth, and looked cross-eyed at the rivulet of rain dripping down the front of her rain hat. "Guess I aint too bright."

"Guess you aint. But I think I'm beginning to like you."

"That's nice to know. Shall we mount up, wagon master?"

The last kilometer was sheer torture. Bent double into the wet blast, we pushed our bikes, struggling for every step. Progress was made more difficult by the unmanageable machines whose rubber tires refused to take purchase on the wet stones, and they would slither and fishtail with every gust of wind. In spite of being carcass-weary, wet to the core, and functioning only on energy fumes, we did manage a rasped-voiced "Hurrah" when we hit the marker signifying Harlingen's city limits.

Thirty minutes later we burst into the lobby of the Zeezicht Hotel.

The desk clerk was an elderly gentleman of refined propriety who blended perfectly with the small but nicely appointed lobby. When he saw the apparition before him, he picked up the spectacles hanging from the chain around his neck, and studied us more closely.

"I want a room for three people," I gargled. "And if you say you're filled up, I'm gonna punch you right in the nose."

The glasses fell to the end of their chain. "Mercy me."

"And I don't want it on the fourth, third, or second floor. If you can't put us on the first floor just roll a couple of cots right into the lobby here. This'll do fine."

"Mercy me!" repeated the clerk. "We do have rooms, yes. Not too many people are traveling in weather like this. I have a nice room on the first floor overlooking the harbor. It's a bit more expensive than—"

"Hang the expense. Hand me the key."

"Very well, sir. If you'll be kind enough to sign the register I'll have a boy park your car and help with the lug——"

"No car. Have him bring the luggage in from our bicycles."

A small, proprietous chuckle escaped through the fingers over his mouth. "You will have to forgive my English. For a moment I thought you said bicycles. Imagine, if you will, bicycling in this weather?"

"Imagine," said Dortha, inadvertently spraying him with rain-hat drips.

"I did say bicycles," I said.

"Bicycles." The desk clerk cleared his voice. "Mercy me. May I ask where you came from on your bicycles?"

"Quatrebras."

"Quatrebras!" There was a clucking sound. "That must be thirty kilometers from here."

"As the crow flies. It's three hundred kilometers when the crow has a strong headwind."

"Mercy me. You certainly must be fatigued. I'll have the boy take care of your bicycles and bring in your luggage. You may sign the register later if you like. Then you won't have to get up off your hands and knees."

One hot shower and two hot buttered rums later, the whole world assumed a much brighter complexion. I sat in a comfortable easy chair, reveling in my own flesh turned from blue to rosy pink, and sipping the hot drink the bellhop had just delivered. Holly was in the shower, and I was watching the wife swishing around in her unmentionables, shaking out our wet clothes. "Certainly is mellow out," I said. "Isn't it, dear?"

She paused in her chore to toast me with her glass. "Mellow as a cello. Nothing in the world like a hot shower and a hot buttered rum when you have icicles on your epiglottis."

"Like to come sit on my lap? Indulge in a little plain and fancy neck-nuzzling?"

"I'm not *that* mellow. And you're not to be trusted. What I really want is something to hang these wet clothes on. You're an ingenious man. Figure something out."

I addressed myself to the problem. My eyes fell on the bungee cords we used to strap the luggage on our bikes. "Ah ha! I have it." I linked the bungees together by their hooks, hooked one end to the window hasp, then stretched the links across the room to fasten the other end to the doorknob. "Voilà, my love! Your very own clothesline."

"Andy!" She threw the wet clothes over the line. "You *are* ingenious."

"True. Now would you like to come and sit on my ingenious lap?"

She took another sip from her drink and cocked her head at me. "Promise to behave yourself?"

"Promise."

"Liar." She sat down on my lap. I pulled her warm, soft, smell-good body close. "You know, love," she said, cuddling up, "this trip has been a real education, hasn't it?"

"In many ways."

"For one, it's made me stand back and look at life from an entirely different perspective. Like today. Our whole confused, mixed-up society we spend so much time worrying about—wars, taxes, politicos, pollution—have become the farthest thing from my mind. I could care less. Out there, today, all alone with the elements, the only thing I thought about was rotating those pedals and wishing cold rain wasn't trickling down my neck." She looked at me. "Isn't that crazy?"

"It's wonderful."

"It's crazy wonderful. But after you've gone through it, it's great therapy. Whenever I get uptight again, worrying about the rat race, I'm going to think of today. And I'm going to remember how simple life really is. And how enjoyable. And how stupid we are to make it such a complex, ulcerating thing."

"Let's drink to that." We touched glasses. "I didn't find today all that enjoyable. In fact, I was downright worried for a short stretch. But I understand what you're saying. And right now, warm, cozy, pooped, and slightly pixilated, I don't think I've ever felt quite so good in my whole, ten-century life."

She smiled. "Me, too." I gave her a long, passionate kiss. She pulled back and gave me a coy look. "You shouldn't be doing that. You'll discharge your pacemaker."

"I brought my pacemaker jump cable. Let's turn 'em up and have a ball."

"Now, Andy—Holly's likely to pop in any minute—"

"Holly's never taken a shower lasting less than two hours in her life. As I see it, we have one hour and forty-five minutes."

"You sure?" She nibbled my ear.

"Positive." I picked up my bride and was halfway to more comfortable surroundings when the door opened.

"Okay," said Holly. "Who's the wise guy who used up all the hot water?"

It wasn't really the interruption of my long-awaited love tryst that bothered me. It was being smacked in the face by a bungee-line full of wet clothes when Holly opened the door.

Sure cools a fellow's ardor.

We fell head over heels in love with Harlingen. The fishing town, situated right on the North Sea, had twice the charm of Cape Cod without any of the tourists and commercialism. The front had passed over, taking the rain with it, and the late afternoon was cool and clearing as we walked through the streets of the canal-stitched town, drinking in the flavor of the beautiful, untrammeled setting. "Look at those great old buildings," I said. "They must be a billion years old."

"At least pre-Raphaelite," said Dortha. "I love the way they all tilt at crazy, fascinating angles."

"The builders in the old days knew how to live. They put far more emphasis on a good, stout tankard of ale than they did a true plumb bob."

"That's not the real reason, Dad," said Holly, surveying the structures critically. "I'd say they're tilted like that due to shifting foundations. The alluvial soil of the lowlands is not conducive to a good bedrock foundation."

I shot a look of disdain at my daughter. "If there's anything I can't stand, it's a college kid."

"Sorry, Pop."

Dortha smiled at me. "I prefer your explanation, honey. I'm sure there's not a word of truth in it, but at least I can understand it."

"Thanks, dear." I stuck my tongue out at Holly. "See that building?" I pointed to a four-storied structure that tilted perilously out over the sound. "With the big bay window on the top floor overlooking the ocean?"

"I see it," said Dortha.

"I want that. That's where I'm going to write the great American novel. Right up there in that loft."

"Better hurry. It's gonna fall into the sea tomorrow."

"Not a chance. It's been there four hundred years. It's good for another century at least. Yes, sir. I'm coming back here some day."

"I'll come with you, Pop," said Holly. "This has got to be the most peaceful spot in the world."

"I'll tag along, too," said Dortha. "Take up painting. If this isn't a painter's paradise, I never saw one."

When we found the seafood restaurant that had been so highly recommended, we were so ravenous we'd have relished sole of old army boot. Instead we had the best sole Bonne Femme we ever hooked a lip over.

After dinner we walked through the harbor, watching a fiery sunset hallucinate the heavens and cast an orange glow over the fishing boats snugged in the harbor. As we returned to the hotel, a fitting cap was put on the day by the appearance of a sport fishing boat, loaded with loaded fishermen. Suffering absolutely no pain, the barley-corned boatmen were trying to coax their twenty-foot-high boat into a canal covered by a nineteen-foot-high bridge. They tried everything short of sawing off the flying bridge—all to no avail. Completely undaunted, however, they solved the enigma by rolling out another keg of

beer and a lengthy inventory of bawdy songs, mixing the two
to while away the hours until the benevolent outgoing tide
came to their aid.

They implored us to join them on deck, especially after
seeing Holly, and as appealing as the idea was, sore muscles
and full-bellied drowsiness dictated otherwise. We declined with
thanks, and went on up to our room. Five seconds later we
were all in bed, and as the sound of well-oiled Dutch sea chan-
ties wafted through the bedroom window, I swore I was positively returning to the enchanting town of Harlingen in the
Netherlands.

Maybe to stay forever.

From the previous day's experience, it became obvious
that bicycle riding and private-plane flying have a lot in com-
mon. Besides both burning lots of fuel, requiring strict attention to proper load and balance, the biggest similarity is the
necessity for an accurate weather forecast.

Old Air Force pilots used to have an axiom that it wasn't
safe to take off until the weight of flight-planning paperwork
equaled the weight of the airplane. And most of this pre-
flight planning was concerned with weather. If the forecast
was bad or marginal, and the mission didn't have a top priority
—like maybe the pilot had a girl friend at his destination—then
everybody either went back to bed or to the bar, to await more
favorable conditions. We also had an old axiom—there are bold
pilots, and there are old pilots. But there are no old bold pilots.
The old pilots went back to the bar and lived to fly another
day.

Having little desire to repeat our treadmill journey of the
previous day, and knowing that winds affect a vehicle traveling fifteen miles an hour far more than one traveling six hundred, I was determined to give more attention to a weather
forecast as a cyclist than I had as a pilot. Particularly on the

upcoming leg of our journey, which promised to be mighty interesting.

The lowlands of Holland are very fertile. Until fairly recently, a large percentage of its fecund farmland had one slight problem, which pretty much hampered proper cultivation: it was under several fathoms of seawater. Unless one wanted to raise shrimp or long-legged cattle, a large hunk of the Netherlands was unproductive. It was this problem a group of Dutch engineers discussed over their cheese fondue one day. Why not build a dam across the northern end of the Zuider Zee? Then pump all that water back into the sea, and reclaim a lot of arable land? Why not, indeed.

Ignoring the pessimists who proved it couldn't possibly be done, the engineers just added a little more kirsch to their fondue and proceeded to build Ijsselmeer Dam, a twenty-mile-long masterpiece of Dutch hydraulic engineering. Ranking in achievement with the building of the pyramids, it was completed in 1932 and became the first step that eventually added more than half a million acres of fertile farmland to the country of Holland. Furthermore, the building of the dam added another fringe benefit, turning the once saline Zuider Zee into a beautiful freshwater lake called Ijsselmeer.

An interesting, if macabre, sidelight to this project has just recently been exposed with the draining of the sea. Some six thousand airplanes shot down over Holland during World War II are being uncovered, and the Dutch are diligently trying to identify the remains of some twelve hundred American airmen who crashed into the Zuider while flying the busy arterial air lane that linked England to Germany during the war.

On the top of this dam the engineers paved a superb roadway, complete with cycle path. It was this route we wanted to take on our journey south through the Netherlands. If the weather were favorable, it could be a grand and glorious cycling experience—one of the highlights of the trip. If it were perverse, it could become sticky, because on that narrow twenty-mile ribbon of earth that kept the sea out of Holland, there was only one place to rest, and it was at the middle of the dam.

Rising early without waking the family, I went down to the desk and roused the snoring night clerk. I explained my problem and enlisted his services in getting the local weather forecast. Very obligingly he called someone on the phone—probably the local service that forecasts for the commercial fishermen—and gave me a full weather report. It looked favorable. The low pressure cell that had given us so much trouble the day before had moved south, and the wind would now be at our back as we headed southwest. Furthermore, no rain was expected.

Routing grumbling troops, we breakfasted, packed, and pushed off into the cool, clear weather. Sleepy dispositions were quickly swept away as we biked along the harbor road, waving at departing fishermen, inhaling the invigorating salt-tang smell of the harbor. I studied the direction of fluttering boat pennants and was glad to see the forecast materializing. In a short time we were out of Harlingen and cycling south through sand-dune country bordering the sea, and then we were at the point where the long dike began.

I scrambled up on a dune and from this vantage point saw the long, narrow corridor of earth shooting into infinity, straight as an arrow. I plucked out my handkerchief, held it up by the corner to catch the breeze. The wind was blowing a brisk twenty knots, directly on our tail. I gave the signal for Bottoms Up.

It was sheer poetry. The fact that we had had to claw for every meter we stuffed under our bicycle tires the day before undoubtedly contributed to the rapture. Sitting up on our bikes as straight as we could to catch the full force of the wind, we literally sailed along, pumping several meters, resting ten. The only sounds were the wheeling gulls, the crashing of the sea on our right, the gentle lapping of the lake on our left, the rapid clicking of our odometers. Puffy cotton cumulus clouds played tag with the sun over our shoulders.

I was completely awed by the feats of the Dutch engineers who had masterminded this amazing dike that was speeding by under our wheels. The world's leaders in hydraulic engineering, the Hollanders had put a tremendous amount of planning into this dam that was keeping the sea from reclaiming their lands—which lie twelve feet below sea level.

We soon became warm, going as fast as the breeze, and we stopped to doff our ponchos. This was when I got the brainstorm.

Sending the troops on ahead while I finished my cigarette, I scouted around until I found several stout sticks. Lashing them into a crude triangle with friction tape from my tool kit, I then covered the frame with the plastic tablecloth. By the time I finished my cigarette I had the makeshift sail mounted on my bicycle. I pedaled to get started, then the wind billowed my sail, and off I went. Leaning back, my feet on the handlebars, I feigned a nap as I sailed serenely by my pumping constituents.

Needless to say, I was the envy of the brood, gliding along with no physical exertion at all, the picture of repose. And then, as so often happens to men of genius, the unexpected happened. I started flushing up seagulls nesting along the dike. They came at me in great clouds, and evidently mistaking me for some kind of strange, winged interloper on their territorial imperative, they started strafing me with raucous cries and processed seafood. I soon had my hands full trying to hold the sail, guide the bicycle, and fend off the fury of flapping feathers.

Then I came under attack from another quarter. The distaff began tossing verbal lambastings about how I should act my age, and she was not going to eat off a tablecloth visited by diarrheic pigeons. Reluctantly I reefed in my sails, muttering under my breath how it's a good thing Orville and Wilbur never had redheaded wives, or we'd all still be crossing oceans on steamships.

In spite of this small frustration, plus frequent stops to admire the beauty, we arrived at the halfway point far ahead of schedule. The midpoint of the dam is marked by a tall monument and a very crowded restaurant. We elbowed through the café to a harried waiter who grudgingly consented to bring us three bottles of apple juice. Then, tiring quickly of being jostled, we beat a hasty exit for the wide-open spaces.

We picnicked in the grass on top of the levee, then, fondled by the cool sea breeze, took a little nap, lulled to sleep by the bickering of the gulls as they finished off our lunch crumbs.

The wind still at our back, it was downhill all the rest of the way to the levee's end. We picked up the bicycle path that paralleled E-10 and floated gaily along to a road juncture at Wieringerwerf, where we came upon one of the poshest roadside motels yet encountered. It easily equaled the best Holiday Inn in the States, with two restaurants, several bars, and luxurious rooms, and I was tempted to splurge for once on hotel accommodations and stay for the night.

The troops quickly brought me to my senses, saying this would be violating our project to see Europe economically, and they would have none of it. Hoping to get some support from the waiter who brought us tea in the dining room, I found even he was against our staying. He confided it was way too expensive, and there was a very charming old hotel just down the road a few kilometers at a little village called Medemblik. He even went to the trouble of getting a map from his car to show us how to get there. This closed the subject.

The trip through this section of rural Holland defies description. Bicycle paths that predate the new highway system

roam through the famous cheese country, whimsically following pretty streams, threading through rich dairy farms, linking tiny villages together. Still feeling fresh after traveling
thirty-eight miles—thanks to the boost from the elements—we
debated stopping at Medemblik. But when we saw the hotel,
the decision to stay was unanimous.

Erected right on a canal at the end of the town's minuscule main street, it could be argued whether the canal came first
or the hotel. It resembled a Rembrandt backdrop, complete
with canting roof, lines that confused geometry, and a facade
held together only by a thousand layers of whitewash. It was
utterly magnificent!

Checking in, we were spirited up to the third floor, a level
we didn't even object to, and ushered into a large, cheery
room with three beds and a floor that tilted grandly at least
twenty degrees to starboard. Just crossing the room presented
the same thrills as the Crazyhouse at the county fair, and I
didn't have to drink a warm Scotch for happy hour that
night. Just trying to pour it was enough to make me tipsy. It
was such a warm and charismatic place we didn't even mind
its original seventeenth-century plumbing. Nor the fact that we
rolled out of bed twice during the night trying to sleep on the
bias. Nor the odd, spasmodic sound that occasionally issued
from the vicinity of the tavern downstairs, sounding like the
wheeze of a valve-stuck calliope just before it exploded. The
latter mystified me, but fearful of what I might find if I in-
vestigated, we just pulled the covers over our heads to spend a
marvelous, if somewhat sleepless, night.

The skies were on the dreary side when I peeked out of
the covers the next morning. Tempted to pull the comforter
back over my head and just let the morning sneak by unobserved, I happened to remember this was the day we were to
meet Scott and his girl friend in Amsterdam. I crawled out
of bed, dressed quietly, and went downstairs for a cup of coffee

to help me screw up the courage to wake the rest of the nomads. Ordering the cup of coffee explained the strange noises during the night.

The magnificent brass coffee maker had more valves than a pipe organ, more wheezing noises than an emphysema victim. It sent out billowing puffs of steam, rocking and rattling the foundation like a gestating volcano, then with one climaxing, orgastic spurt it plopped out a glob of liquid lava into a waiting cup. Drunk straight, this elixir was excellent for performing tonsillectomies. Mixed half with hot milk, it made one hell of a cup of coffee.

Properly fortified, I roused the troops, we reclaimed our bikes from the kitchen where the staff had stored them for safekeeping, and loaded up. The weather didn't seem to be improving, and the forecast called for possible showers. I made the decision to head for the nearest depot.

Ascertaining the closest one was at Hoogkarspel, some ten clicks away, we started out in threatening skies. After a half hour the threat became a reality, and we were soon pumping through a light drizzle. The wind was not kicking up, however, and the ponchos protected us from the rain. We enjoyed the early morning ride to Hoogkarspel. Especially knowing we wouldn't have to put up with sloppy weather all day.

We had little trouble finding the depot at Hoogkarspel, but the stationmaster turned out to be a problem. Through patient sign language he told us we could ride his train but our bikes could not. There was no baggage car. The closest depot that would take our bikes was at Hoorn, another twelve clicks down the road.

We again took to the trail. Even dribbling skies did not mar the pleasant trip through the large "Wieringermeerpolder," a 45,000-acre "polder," or territory, reclaimed from the Zuider Zee. As we cycled toward the old town of Hoorn we traversed the locales of the world's great cheeses—Edam and Alkmaar—

dating back to the year 800. Here is the colorful cheese market at the Weigh-house, which has been captured on the emulsion of a million cameras. We breezed over delightful canal draw-bridges and had a rest break in the shelter of a groaning wind-mill, one of three hundred used occasionally, out of a thousand that still stand in Holland as silent reminders of years gone by.

A head wind started kicking up, and we were glad to pull into Hoorn, to follow the railroad tracks to the depot. Here the bikes were received with open arms, and an obliging train schedule provided a waiting train at the platform to whisk us the short distance to Amsterdam.

We shared our compartment with several Dutch college kids going to the big city for a holiday, and they insisted on sharing with us the best-tasting cheese ever made, along with a loaf of fresh Dutch bread and several huge bottles of native Holland beer.

It was one of the better lunches, and I wasn't the only one who didn't particularly care whether the train ever arrived in Amsterdam or not.

Unfortunately, it did.

10

You Don't Shoot a Bicycle with a Broken Spoke

AMAZING Amsterdam! The chief trading port on the continent that links with Indonesia and Dutch Guiana and exotic lands of the world. The cosmopolitan city of canals and bridges and chic couturiers and Rembrandt and art treasures galore. Little wonder it nudges Copenhagen as one of Europe's most fascinating cities.

As one cruises its canals that break the city up into a hundred islands, and gazes in breath-sucking wonder at the gilded patrician mansions and former homes now converted into business establishments, at the flowers and parks everywhere, at the genteel, dignified Amsterdam way of life—one is apt to forget the history of this hedonistic city.

It was built on the carcasses of herrings. Its very existence is due to its early mastery of the capture of a fish homely to the eye but pleasing to the palate. The city itself personifies the "Golden Age" of the Netherlands, when the seventeenth century saw Holland as one of the world's leading powers after emerging the winner of the bloody Eighty Years' War with

Spain. A person might be hard-pressed to find wooden shoes, or working windmills, or even a tulip bulb in twentieth-century Amsterdam. Nor could we find many young ice skaters with swollen thumbs from plugging dike holes. But we found other things. Including one son.

Scott was standing on the fringe of flower children wilting around the entrance to the American Express office in downtown Amsterdam. He looked and felt miserable. He was broke, hungry, had a bad cold and a worse disposition. He had spent nearly a week and all his money in Copenhagen awaiting Betty Jo. He had met every plane, only to find out via a letter delivered at the American Express office on the last day that she intended to arrive at Amsterdam. Due in day after tomorrow. "And to top it all off," concluded Scott, "someone stole the tire pump off my bike."

I was not the sympathetic father I should have been. I lit into him. Leaving no doubt as to my feelings about a young buck stupid enough to let some dame ruin his trip to Europe, who would blow all his money, not eat right, ruin his resistance and catch cold, and not show responsibility for his personal property.

"Thanks, Dad," he said. "I've got some kind of bug. I've been vomiting all morning. I really needed that."

As usual, Dortha the mediator took over. "We'll get some food into you, Scott. You'll feel better. Andy, why don't you get us a hotel room?"

I grumbled off in search of a phone, my mood matching Scott's. I hated the idea of Scott's glorious trip to Europe being ruined by some frustrating female. I hated myself even more for acting the cantankerous-father role. Scott was an adult, as he often pointed out, and it was high time our father-son relationship graduated to a person-to-person basis. Vowing to be more flexible in the future, I found a phone, turned to Art Frommer's section on Amsterdam, and chased down hotel rooms.

The Hotel de Moor on Prinsengracht Street was a rare find. Centrally located and clean as a surgeon's scalpel, it was managed by a brother and sister who had inherited it and who were completely dedicated to making their guests as comfortable as humanly possible. All for ten dollars a night for the four of us, breakfast included.

We had scheduled several days in Amsterdam to give us a chance to rest up, do the laundry, pick up the mail, and give the pride a chance to see this fabulous city. The first afternoon was spent in ministering to Scott's maladies. Dortha presided over him with much tongue-clucking sympathy, while keeping me at arm's length lest I start fanning smoldering embers. Following a hot bath and clothes freshened at the local laundromat, it turned out that his main problem was caused by hunger pangs.

As evidenced by the amount of food he put away at a nearby Indonesian restaurant.

When the Dutch East Indies were part of Holland's empire, the Dutch imported an Indonesian heartburn delight called Rijsttafel (rice table). This deglutition adventure involves a heaping bowl of rice placed before each diner, in which are dunked delicacies that keep coming for hours. They range from smoked eel to roast pork on sticks to vegetables in peanut sauce to fried bananas and coconut—most of which are spiced with seasoned napalm. And contributing greatly to the delight of eating Rijsttafel is the necessity of quenching the fire with great drafts of Dutch beer.

After going through twenty courses of this epicurean gastritis even Scott was getting filled up, and we rolled, rather than walked, back to the hotel.

All in all, Rijsttafel is a delightful, you-gotta-do-it-at-least one-time, three-Alka-Seltzer experience. What's more, it's not fattening, for I found its excess calories were more than burned off by making at least three double-time trips to the john before daybreak.

The next morning, in spite of her abdominal arson, the distaff was in a good mood. Whenever she scratched my back before we got out of bed it was a suspicious sign. And when she followed this with a Swedish massage, I knew my worst fears were about to surface.

They did, over soft-boiled eggs at breakfast. I was in formed, quite matter-of-factly, that this was the day we were going to spend with the muses. "The whole family is going to absorb a little culture," she said, looking at me, "even if it kills us. We are going to visit the Amsterdam art museums. Amsterdam is called the largest open-air museum in the world, and today we're going to see it."

Before I could marshal my defenses, I found myself standing in front of No. 4 Jodenbreestraat, the home of Rembrandt van Rijn.

I have never been a particularly rabid art buff. To show the extent of my art appreciation, I used to think George Petty and Charles Russell were pretty good, and when I saw Grant Wood's *American Gothic* I was quite content to let my artistic education end right there. As a consequence, I could think of at least a dozen places I would rather be in Amsterdam on a nice, sunny morning than at the doorstep of Rembrandt's house.

But that was before I entered.

I no sooner crossed the threshold of the elegant digs where Rembrandt lived, than I became totally immersed in the weird twists of fate that coiled around this fascinating genius. In fact, upon learning Rembrandt was forced to give up this beautiful seventeenth-century home because of bankruptcy, and the bankruptcy was caused by one painting, I was the one who urged us all to search it out.

We found it at the Rijksmuseum, acknowledged as one of the continent's greatest art museums. Here, highlighted among the brilliant masterworks of Dutch painters, is the *Night Watch*. One of the most controversial canvases ever painted, even its title could not be agreed upon—some calling it *The Company of Captain Frans Banning Coq and Lieutenant Willem van Ruytenburgh*. Although claimed by some as the greatest painting of all time, it was such a different vision of a group of men, and Captain Coq's troops raised so much hell, that all Amsterdam looked on it as a disaster. As a result, paintings by Rembrandt fell into immediate disfavor, and he packed up his brushes and beat it to the poorer Rozengracht area where he evaded his creditors by working in his son's art firm, and lived out his days with his mistress, Hendrickje Stoffels, a plump little Dutch dumpling.

Still reeling with the inequities of the artistic world, we found ourselves being shepherded to 263 Prinsengracht, better known as the house of Anne Frank.

The diary of the fourteen-year-old girl who spent two years hiding from the Nazis has been told in books of every language, on the stage, and in film. But to personally visit the secret annex behind the bookcase that conceals the stairway to the upstairs apartment where Anne lived; to see the yellowed clippings preserved there—a photo of Deanna Durbin, other mementos that throbbed the heart of any teen-ager; to feel the claustrophobic two-year terror of being given away by so little as a flushing toilet—is to relive the most gross horror of man's inhumanity to man.

As one proceeds through the house, a cauldron of emotions bubbles up—excruciating sadness, disbelief, fury—yet, as you leave the house and read an excerpt from Anne's diary on the door, your mood is elevated. It reads: "In spite of everything, I still believe that people are really good at heart. If I look up into the heavens, I think that it will all come right, that this cruelty too will end, and that peace and tranquility will return again."

It is a sober, searing, tearful experience.

It wasn't until we had basked in the atmosphere of a marvelous old Dutch-doored tavern named *The Glorie*, on Kerkstraat, that our solemnity was dissipated—with the help of delightful surroundings and a satisfied inner man. Once again we were grateful for the advice of Art Frommer, who recommended the delicious kitchen and old-world atmosphere of The Glorie over the overrated and overpriced famous Five Flies restaurant of Amsterdam. With a delectable two-dollar dinner of steak and mushrooms under our belt, we took a leisurely roundabout stroll back to the hotel, where we relaxed and made plans for the next leg of our journey.

One of Dortha's missions on the European trip was to visit her brother's grave at the United States Military Cemetery at Margraten, just a few miles from Maastricht in Holland. Merle Power, a handsome, gentle young man—and one of my favorite people—had been a lieutenant in the Fifth Armored Division during World War Two. He had been killed in a military engagement near Aachen, Germany.

The intervening years since Merle's death had left deep scars on Dortha's family, which had very nearly capsized at the news thirty years ago. It had been particularly hard on Dortha, who had been very close to her brother, especially since she had been in Europe working for the Red Cross when the tragedy occurred.

It had been decided to bury Merle in the Netherlands, rather than go through the double agony of bringing his remains back to the States. As with most servicemen buried in Holland, Merle's grave had been adopted by a Dutch family who tended it, placed flowers on it during frequent visits, and provided a liaison with Dortha's folks in the States. Throughout the years this splendid Dutch clan had kept in touch with Dortha's mother, and this charitable act had been a ray of sunshine in the dark gloom of mourning.

We had visited Merle's grave during our last visit to Holland; when the sprawling, cross-studded American cemetery had been little more than a dismal, heart-wrenching sea of mud. At the same time we had looked up the Dutch family to pay our respects, and to thank them sincerely for a kindness it would be impossible to repay.

And now Dortha had the sad but compelling mission ahead of her, to again visit the grave of her brother. It was decided she would go alone, leaving on the train from Amsterdam the next day. Betty Jo—providing she made her flight— would then take Dortha's bicycle and ride with the youngsters and me to Brussels, where we would all rejoin.

The next day plans fell into shape. Scott came back from the airport with a pretty, big-eyed, shapely brunette on his arm; he was a man lifted from the depths of despair to hypoxic altitudes by the arrival of his Betty Jo. She was bubbling with contriteness and apologies for having fouled up her arrival. Scott, lying through his teeth, was dismissing it as of entirely no consequence, inasmuch as his waiting periods had been occupied by the passionate commiseration of dozens of golden-tressed, blue-eyed Norwegian and Dutch girls.

Gagging at this ghastly display of guiltless guile, Big Red and I shooed them all out. Scott and Betty Jo left in search of some secluded corner where they could catch up on their mooning and lip-lashing; Holly set off for the Stedelijk Museum to give Van Gogh a go.

Dortha was in a rare, quiet mood. She had mixed feelings about her upcoming trip. She wanted to go, but she hated traveling alone. Furthermore, she was genuinely sorry about missing part of our cycling journey through Holland. Hoping to cheer her up, I suggested we go to the Floriad, the spectacular flower exposition just outside Amsterdam. I didn't need to repeat the offer, as Dortha's love of flowers is exceeded only by her love of homemade fudge. In a flash we were on the trolley heading for the Floriad.

It was worth the trip. Even I, who always associated flowers with funerals, hospitals, and expensive corsages, was smitten by the acres of exotic blooms and plants from all over the world. Dortha's morale improved with every bloom, and by dusk she was her old ebullient self. Arriving back at the hotel, we were happy to find a note saying the offspring were taking Betty Jo to dinner at an Indonesian restaurant. This provided a rare opportunity for the old poops to have a night on the town alone.

While the redhead was still in rapture over the rhododendrons, I decided to splurge and take her to the Pied de Cochon, a nearby French restaurant recommended by the hotel manager as being *par excellence*. It was a candlelit converted wine cellar that fairly reeked with romantic atmosphere. Feeling very devilish, we ordered a couple of genevers, the Dutch gin made from war-surplus torpedo propellant, before dinner. The waiters made a big production of bringing in cognac-splashed steaks on flaming swords, and we made a big production of holding our breath lest the flame ignite the fumes of genevers, to dissolve the whole restaurant in a blazing holocaust.

After a wine-fortified dinner that will stand out forever in our memories of fabulous feasts, we banked the coals with an afterdinner Advokaat, a heavily spiked eggnog affair eaten with a spoon. You eat it quickly, before the spoon dissolves.

The world was never rosier as we left the restaurant and decided to take a moonlight canal ride. We climbed into one of the quiet, glass-domed launches and started gliding through another world of illuminated canals and bridges, past facades of marvelous old buildings bathed in the glow of soft lights.

Listening to the boat's romantic stereo music, munching cheese and drinking wine served by a long-stemmed stewardess, we drifted through the fairyland of Amsterdam after dark—I making improper advances, Dortha skillfully fending them off without spilling so much as a drop of her wine.

It was an evening we both wished could go on forever.

Bright and early the next morning I saw Dortha onto her train. "Now don't talk to strangers," I said, putting her suitcase in the overhead rack. "And keep your money pinned in your bra. You sure you don't need anything?"

"Just you, love." She took my hand. "Sorry about last night. I never dreamed the kids would get home so early."

"The story of my life. I'm giving up sex, anyway. As the man says, it's highly overrated, underwhelming, and the position is ridiculous. Besides, I think my ovaries are drying up."

She smiled. "That'll be the day."

"That's not my only problem. I've got to chaperone three college kids for the next three days. I'll be spending all my time flushing Scott and Betty Jo out of bushes. I think you're terrible to take off and leave me at a time like this."

She looked into my eyes, her face solemn. "Do you really?"

I smiled at her. "Of course I don't, honey."

"It's nothing that just *has* to be done. I hate traveling by myself. And you know how I'm going to miss you and my ding-dong family—"

"It's only for three short days. And we both know you'd never forgive yourself if you missed this opportunity. You owe it to yourself, your family, and especially that white-haired mother of yours. What's more, I have a feeling Merle just might appreciate it, too."

She put her arms around my neck. "You know what, you big ox?"

"What's what?"

"I love you. I really do."

We kissed like teen-agers until the train started to move. Then I raced out of the compartment and waved from the platform until the train was out of sight.

In Amsterdam there are 850,000 people and 400,000 bicycles. We met them all as we shouldered through the morning crowds on their way to work. My young adults were in a happy mood, Scott and Betty Jo in their own little nauseating world, Holly glowing with anticipation. She had received a letter from Erik Swenson, the young soldier she had met in Sweden, saying his leave had been approved, and he was looking forward to meeting her in Brussels. At least the morale of the troops was in fine shape.

The bike roads were marvelous, even more sophisticated than any we had seen. Their Lilliputian signal lights guided the two-wheeled traffic effortlessly and safely through the clanging trams, speeding vehicles, and high-powered motorcycles that were forbidden to use the bike trails. Betty Jo, her long, athletic legs pumping easily, had no trouble acclimating to Dortha's bike, and kept up easily.

Out of the city limits and established on the road leading to Utrecht, we stopped for a breather. I tested the wind with my handkerchief, found we were going to have a following wind and clear sailing. The sun came out, sparkling the canal that paralleled the bike trail, making it a very splendid morning.

As we started up again, my thoughts were diverted from Dortha's lonely pilgrimage by a bumping in the vicinity of my rear wheel. Investigating, I found my rear tire was flat. I used the bicycle pump for the first time, rode on a way—only to find the tire flat again. I obviously had a puncture. According to the map, there was a little village about a mile off our course.

It just might have a bicycle shop. We turned off and headed down a country lane.

The tiny hamlet had a bike repair shop. We had arrived at noon, however, and the place was closed for lunch. We bought a bottle of milk, produced our sandwiches, and were just about to sit down on the curb and eat when the shop owner's wife beckoned to us from the side of the store. Following her, she led us into a little garden that was part of her house behind the bicycle shop. Here she had set a place for us. Lawn chairs surrounded a little table, which had been furnished with a table-cloth and a bowl of fruit. We munched away in the delightful garden, surrounded by several precocious children, two friendly cats, an amiable goat that liked to eat milk cartons, and a bee-hive of bees—which Betty Jo watched with nervous apprehension.

We finished lunch just as the shop owner finished fixing my tire. I paid the ridiculous fifty-cent bill and included a tip for the proprietor which produced a large smile; then I grandly kissed the shop owner's wife on the hand, producing a parox-ysm of giggles. We had solved our first bike problem by the removal of a sharp rock from the rear tire.

Back on course, and wheeling merrily along an hour later, we found that mishaps, like grapes, seem to come in bunches. This time Holly's tire sprang a leak. Adding to the predicament, in checking my map I found we were miles from the nearest village. This required truly drastic measures. Such as trying to utilize the tire repair kit in our toolcases, with the instructions written only in French.

None of us had ever removed a bicycle tire before, let alone tried to fix an inner tube. And now, as usual, whenever our bicycle wheels came to rest, Scott and Betty Jo disap-peared into the nearest thicket. This left Holly and me to try and figure out how to mend an incapacitated bicycle. We finally located the villain—a small nail—removed it, and after a twenty-minute bout managed to beat the tire into submission and remove it from the wheel. Another twenty minutes was expended in removing the inner tube from the tire, then all we had to do was take a crash course in French so we could read the instructions on the tire repair kit.

It took a half hour of trial, error, and total recall from my old Model T Ford days before finally stumbling upon the correct sequence of applying the tiny patch to the tube. At last we found the patch stuck to the tube long enough to insert it back into the tire, and remounted the tire on the wheel. As I pumped it up—finding to our vast relief it was holding air—I sent Holly off to round up the lovers.

When they returned, Betty Jo noticed the tire-repair kit as I was stuffing the tools back into their case. She picked it up and started reading in flawless French.

"Don't tell me you know French!" I sputtered.

"Very well," she said. "It's my language major. Why?"

I checked myself. It would never do for the wagon master to show any signs of stress or emotional instability. I addressed my son. "For the rest of this mission we're going to spend less time necking in the bushes and more time at our battle stations!" So saying, I shot my son my sternest look, and mounted up.

"One question, Dad?" asked Scott.

"What is it?" I snapped.

"Why are you riding off on Holly's bicycle?"

In clusters, like grapes.

During this one day we reaped more misfortune than we had during the whole trip. The third mishap occurred as we were passing through the little town of Breukelen. Scott and Betty Jo were riding abreast up ahead, when Scott decided to plant a kiss on his girl friend. It was quite an admirable feat of balance and dexterity, until Scott, never one to do things half-way, decided to put his heart and soul into it. He might have gotten away even with this, had he not stuck his foot in Betty Jo's spokes in the process. There was brief indecision on the part of the bicycle, as if wondering how to cope with a foot in the spokes. Then it decided to take refuge in a hedge bordering the bike trail. The bike jammed into the hedge and stopped. Betty Jo, alas, did not. Instead of Scott, she was suddenly kissing the roadbed.

It was a bad spill.

I hurried up, fear gnawing my innards. Betty Jo was stunned, but a cursory examination showed no major damage. Scott was hovering over her, apoplectic with apology, threatening to kill himself for such stupidity. I volunteered to help him, then went over and extracted the bicycle from the hedge. I was shattered. The fork embracing the front wheel was twisted to a thirty-degree angle. The front wheel itself had developed characteristics more oval than circular. Holly, appearing at my side, looked down in horror at the mutilated machine. "Baby!" she said, stroking its crooked handlebars. "Speak to me."

Betty Jo, who had stirred to a sitting position on the ground, took one look and moaned. "Oh, my God! Look at Mrs. Anderson's bike. She'll skin me alive!"

"Not you, Betty Jo," I said. "But I wouldn't give two cents for your boyfriend's epidermis." The compassion in my heart turned to blood in my eye. I turned to my son and bore in. "Scott, all the world does not necessarily love a lover. From this instant on I want you to quit mooning over Betty Jo like some splay-gaited, love-starved puppy. Start acting your age!" I looked at Scott cowering on the sidewalk, and immediately hated myself for the emotional outburst. "Holly, let's you and I go find a bicycle repair shop."

Holly pointed across the street. "How about that one?"

Luck sometimes forms an amalgam with tragedy. Gathering up the twisted frame in my arms, I swallowed a lump in my throat, and marched stoically across the street, Holly accompanying me. "Let's just pray," I said, "we don't have to shoot it."

Tenderly I laid the carcass at the feet of the small Dutchman who ran the cycle shop. He spoke no English, but it made no difference. Reading the story in my eyes, he moved to a large clock on the wall, pointed to the figure four, picked up the remains and disappeared into the back room.

There was nothing to do now but wait.

We utilized the time by locating a hotel. As it would be late when the bike was ready, and out of deference to Betty Jo's condition, I thought it would be prudent to cave in early. Spurning suggestions to see a doctor, she affirmed she was a little sore, but nothing at all serious. The troops went on to the hotel, Scott stopping to get some medicine to relieve the pain (with bruised ribs should you get a bottle of red or white wine?), and at four o'clock I picked up the bicycle.

As further testimony to a fine machine, I was amazed to find it as good as new. The wheels were once again circular, the fork straight. Even previous scratches had been touched up. The diminutive Dutchman was very apologetic about the bill, gesticulating that two men had put in two hours apiece working on it. I dismissed the whole thing with a generous wave of my hand, paid the seven dollars, and rode the bike back to the hotel.

We had a good dinner at the hotel restaurant, and went up to our rooms early. I convinced Scott an all-night vigil at Betty Jo's bedside was not really necessary, for if appetite was any indication of health, the groceries she stowed at dinner would certainly see her removed from the critical list. He grunted his acquiescence and went with me to our room, the girls going to theirs.

An unaccustomed frosty silence ensued between us as we

readied to retire. I tried reading in bed for awhile, gave up and turned out my bedlamp. I noticed Scott's cigarette glowing in the dark. I cleared my throat. "We had an old saying in the Air Force. 'He who smokes in bed sooner or later makes an ash of himself.' "

The butt was snuffed out. "Yes, Father."

"I guess I'm being a bit of a bastard, aren't I?"

Silence.

"I apologize for the verbal whiplash after the accident this afternoon. A first-class wagon master wouldn't have lost his cool."

"I had it coming."

"Not in front of other people you didn't. First thing I learned as an officer. Praise in public, condemn in private. I did a stupid thing. I'm asking you to accept my apology."

"No apology necessary. It was my stupidity that started the whole thing." He rolled over and pulled up his covers. "Mind if we talk about it some other time?"

"Some other time, son."

It took me a long time to get to sleep. Before finally dropping off I swore I was going to find a school somewhere that gave a refresher course on The Art of Being a Father.

Fortunately, there's something very therapeutic about bicycle riding. Whether it's the heady flush of good exercise, the sensation of being as close to the beauties of nature as one can get, or the sense of complete, freewheeling independence, the breeze generated by one's own physical exertion has the happy faculty of blowing away grudges, bad moods, grumpy feelings, and all hostilities.

And so it was the following morning when we resumed our progress toward Brussels. It was a cool, bright day in mid-September that fostered soaring spirits as we mounted the country road lined with towering trees on one side, a broad navigable canal on the other. The tensions of the day before were forgotten as we breezed by beautiful mansions overlooking the great, rambling estates and stopped to investigate a marvelous old Gothic castle. We had a midmorning coffee break watching an ancient windmill grind grain.

Toward late morning we started playing tag with a handsome cruiser on the canal that was bearing a couple toward the city. They were cruising at a majestic ten knots, and we took turns passing each other, finding, in spite of our frequent stops, that we were making better time than the cruiser. Finally, in a lighthearted spurt of energy to demonstrate the advantage of the rotating bike pedal over the reciprocating marine engine, we took off in a burst of speed and left them in the dust.

We passed through Utrecht and stopped for lunch on the outskirts of town, hanging our feet over the wall of a canal lock. Just as we were getting into our cheese and fruit, the lock gates opened to admit none other than our tag-playing cruiser, and we managed to split a bottle of wine with its gregarious occupants before the water rose to sluice them out the other end.

I had spotted a small village named Hank on the map. Feeling that a town named Hank should never be passed up, and since its geographical location would realize a good day's ride, this was to be our destination for the night. We were distressed to find upon arrival that Hank did not have a hotel. Nor did two other villages on down the line. We were advised that Raamsdonksveer, eight kilometers down the road, did have accommodations. We had already traveled more than fifty miles, so this meant a rough day, particularly for Betty Jo, who was not in quite as good condition as the rest of us. She was a game sport, however, and we struck off.

It was a motley-looking crew that eventually confronted the hotel clerk at the Huis Ten Deyl Hotel in Raamsdonksveer and asked for accommodations. We were all dusty, the girls dressed in patched jeans (great for bike riding, but something less than sartorially splendid), and Scott wearing a beard and an old Swedish battle jacket he had liberated from the Amsterdam flea market. It took a bit of persuasion on my part to convince the desk clerk we weren't some spinoff branch of the Hell's Angels, that I was the responsible patriarch of this peregrinating commune, and that one should not judge a book by its cover.

We were taken in. In more ways than one. I must not have been too successful in stating my case, for we were provided rooms in the loft that would have been dwarfed by an airline lavatory. With beds that pulled down out of the wall.

We dined at a Chinese restaurant named the Pretty Palace, and I spent the rest of the night listening to Scott talking in his sleep and tossing on his egg roll, and trying to keep my bed from folding back into the wall with me in it.

I missed my wife. And I couldn't help wondering how she was getting along all by herself on her lonely, sad journey.

11

People Suffering from Cyclemania Are Cyclepathic

IT'S difficult to get an early start when dragging three preening longhairs. Why it takes so long in the morning to get ready to look the way they end up looking is one of the mysteries of the ages.

We were behind schedule, due to Betty Jo's accident. We were to meet Dortha in Brussels on the morrow. I had hoped to make the city by evening to nail down a hotel room for her arrival, and we had a long way to go. Responding sluggishly to my chafings, the caravan did manage to hit the trail before midmorning. The prognostication of scattered showers came true, one hitting us just in time for coffee break. Over a cup of hot chocolate we waited for it to pass, then thrust out again into growling skies.

The next shower that hit us was not a shower. It was a full-blown storm, accompanied by banshee winds and dancing lightning. Caught unsheltered, we were quickly drenched to the scuppers, sliding around on slippery cobblestones, cold to the marrow. I called a confab in the shelter of a bus stop and consulted the map.

We were very close to Breda.

Breda was a nice little city with a nice dry depot with nice dry trains that ran in and out. I didn't need a show of hands to decide if we should take one.

We spent the next couple of hours watching the rain streak down the windows of a nice warm train, rather than down the lenses of our glasses. We were in Brussels by midafternoon.

The siblings had planted broad hints that it might be nice for them to stay at a hostel in Brussels, where Betty Jo was to meet a girl friend coming in from the States. I surprised them by giving my enthusiastic approval, knowing they were as tired of being chaperoned as I was of being the chaperone. Accordingly, after we checked the bikes in the station baggage room, we scouted out the tourist bureau, obtained reservations for the youth hostelers, and found a room for me. I had hoped to get into the Rembrandt Hotel, a favored small hotel where I was to meet Dortha the next day, but the last room had just been taken. I settled for a small pension a block away.

We separated, the troops gamboling off through the rain, kicking up their heels like young colts let out to pasture. I hailed a taxi and went to my lodgings. There I ordered two beers brought up to the room; then I showered, caught up on my notes, and started heeding hunger pangs. As I dressed for dinner, I felt unaccountably lonely. On my way to a nearby restaurant I dropped by the Rembrandt Hotel to see if I could make reservations for Dortha's arrival the next night. As I passed the hotel's restaurant on the way to the lobby, I did a double take.

There, sitting near the window, a cup of tea halfway to her lips, was my favorite wife.

I reached her mouth before her cup did, in an embrace

that caused silverware all over the restaurant to drop. "You're not supposed to be here until tomorrow night," we said in unison.

I flagged the waiter, requesting he take the tea away and replace it with something a little more spirited. As he obliged, I explained why we had gotten in early, and why I was alone.

"I had good train connections," she said. "I checked in here at the Rembrandt late this afternoon. Got the last room."

"So you're the one! I tried, but some nogoodnik took the last room. I'm staying at the Avia, a block from here."

"Oh, no!"

"And I can't check out 'cause I've already used the shower and made a shambles of the room."

"I can't either. I took a nap in my bed. Talk about planning. Big reunion. We finally get rid of the kids for a night, and we have rooms in two different hotels."

I squeezed her hand. "Don't worry. We'll work something out. Tell me about your trip."

"I'll be happy to. If you'll buy me something to eat."

"You got a deal." We ordered, and as we ate she talked about her journey.

Her train had taken her to Maastricht, where she stayed the first night; then she took a bus to the cemetery at Margraten. She was completely overwhelmed by the transformation the cemetery had undergone. Lush lawn had replaced mud, the grounds were beautifully landscaped, flowers and trees were in abundance. She had picked up some fresh flowers for the grave, and had spent most of the day there. What she had dreaded as a sad, soul-wrenching experience had turned out to be a day of peaceful, lovely communion with her brother.

"Then you're glad you went," I said, when she had finished.

"I can't tell you how glad. And it's going to be so gratifying to report to the family that Merle is resting in such a beautiful place. For Mom, especially, it will do wonders."

"I couldn't be more pleased."

"So. My trip was heavenly. Literally. How was yours?"

I looked pained. "Next time I'm going with you. Ever tried to chaperone two lovesick college kids in the age of sexual permissiveness? I think I chased them out of very bush, haystack, and windmill between here and Amsterdam. I'm like the eunuch who got fired. I'm just not cut out for this type of work."

She laughed. "Was it really that bad, love?"

"I'll spare you the grislies. And you should try sleeping with Scott some time." I grabbed her hand. "Promise me. Promise me you'll never leave me again."

She breathed huskily in my ear. "I promise, husband. I'll never leave you again. Now take me home."

"Will I ever!"

We skipped up to the hotel desk at the Rembrandt, and Dortha asked for her key. The man behind the desk smiled at Dortha, handed her the key, then his eyes fell on me. The smile faded. Dortha, noting the look I was getting, hastened to explain. "Oh, this is my husband. He just arrived. He's staying at another hotel."

"Your husband?" The smile faded, then turned upside down. "He's staying at another hotel?"

"It's a long story," said Dortha, smiling disarmingly. "He's coming up to my room for a minute, then going back to his hotel." We started for the elevator. The lift was not enclosed; I saw his eyes following me all the way up to the third floor.

We burst into her room. "Aha!" I said, slamming the door. "I've got you in my power. Just the two of us here. Me. You. Just us two. In a hotel room. All to ourselves. Just you and me. No kids. Nobody. Just Dortha and Andy. All alone. Hot damn!" I tackled her and threw her on the bed. "Let's make hickeys."

"Hey, hey! My husband with the subtle approach. You really know how to sweep a girl off her feet."

"Don't talk. Pucker."

"Just watch it, Charlie." She pushed me back.

"Whaddaya mean, watch it Charlie?"

"That's what I mean. One kiss. Then you're going to pack up your puckerer and leave. Like a good boy."

"My love for you is making the blood boil in my head. I'm not hearing right."

"You're hearing right." She gave me a long, loving kiss. "Now, out!"

"That kiss was a nice hors d'oeuvre. Now let's get down to the main course."

"That was the main course." She pushed me off the bed. "Thanks for the lovely dinner. Now, if you don't mind, I don't entertain men in my room." She went to the door and opened it. "It's been fun."

"You're kidding!" I stared at her in disbelief. "No, you're not kidding."

"I'm not kidding. A woman has her reputation to maintain."

"Honey, I love a gag, but this is prepos——"

"You saw the look the desk clerk gave us. He's thinking evil thoughts. He saw me check in alone. Then a couple hours later I come in with a tall, handsome stranger. This is a respectable hotel. Didn't you see the sign over the desk?" She framed it with her hands. " 'This is a respectable hotel.' I wouldn't be surprised if the vice squad is on its way up this minute."

"Now hold on! You're overlooking one small detail. I happen to be your husband." I produced my wallet. "Look. My driver's license. Name's same as yours. Anderson. See?"

"Makes no difference. I'd like to snuggle with you all night. But this isn't the night. If the vice squad doesn't show up, the hotel manager will. I'm only paying for a single room. Two can't sleep in it. Now give me a goodnight kiss on your way out."

Stupefied, I obliged. "Well, I'm a sonuva——"

"No you're not. You're a darling man, and I love you dearly. Good night." Then I was out in the hall, the door closed behind me. While I stared at it in a state of shock, the bolt snapped shut.

In a daze I walked down the three flights. Passing the desk, I glanced at the clerk. The frown had been replaced by a beatific smile. "Lovely night, Mr. Anderson. After all that rain. Unbelievable."

"Unbelievable," I said, heading for the door, "is hardly the word."

In my judgment, Brussels is the least appealing of any of the European capitals. Especially after visiting Copenhagen and Amsterdam. If one is content merely to quaff from the cup of history, one can go on a real binge in this city. If one is not historically inclined, the high spots can be covered easily in one day.

The following day we proved it. In the morning Dortha checked out of her respectable hotel and we set out to see the sights. La Grand' Place the huge square which houses the un-touched ancient guild halls of the Middle Ages, is worthwhile, but doesn't hold a candle to Venice's Piazza San Marco; the whole battlefield of Waterloo could be stuck into one revet-ment of our Gettysburg; and the famous "vulgar" Manneken-Pis is about as exciting as a baby brother.

The latter did, however, provide the highlight of the day, as the little piddling prince was dressed in a mailman's uni-form. In honor of Postman's Day, the little fellow did create quite a sensation among the tourists as he graphically illus-trated what a lot of people think about today's mail service.

The day was also active for the younger set. Betty Jo elected to forego bicycling in favor of Eurailpassing it with her girl friend, Helen, who showed up at the American Embassy. Scott was shattered. The girls' plan to rejoin us in Calais, France, didn't even cheer him up. While his morale plummeted to new lows, Holly's soared to new heights, as Erik Swenson materialized as promised—all eight hundred pounds. I sighed. For the moment we could quit worrying about Scott's problems and start worrying about Holly's.

The next morning the troops took a walking tour of the city, I paid bills picked up with the mail at the American Express Office, and Dortha set out with her laundry bag. I picked her up at noon, just as three assorted, smiling Belgians were folding the laundry into her bag.

"That your wife?" I turned to the source of the query. I beheld a good-looking young American with nice teeth he was not ashamed of.

"As a matter of fact, it is."

"You're a lucky man."

"Lucky? I never really looked at it quite that way."

"I like her. She had a little trouble understanding the Belgian laundromats. I ran the washers for her."

"I'm not at all surprised."

"She tells me you folks are cycle touring. I am, too."

I was immediately taken by the young man. Especially when I found out he had spent three months seeing Europe on bikes with his girl friend. He was the first American cyclist we had run across, and I invited him to have lunch with us. He accepted before I finished the question.

Over a steaming plate of mussels—Brussels' excellent contribution to gourmandism—I found out his name was Bill Morgan, he was from Santa Clara, California, was a real bike nut, and had cycled extensively through Switzerland.

"The Alps!" I gasped. "You cycled over the Alps?"

"My girl friend and I. She's not with me now. Had to get back to her job. But it was emphatically the greatest part of our trip. And it's not nearly as bad as it sounds. You been to Switzerland?"

"Yes."

"Then you know the roads don't all go straight up and down over the mountains. They pretty much follow the river-beds, which cut through the ranges. There are some steep climbs, of course, but I have a special alpine gear on my bike, and they presented no real problem. If you get tired, which we did once, you can throw your bike on one of the cog trains and whisk right up to the top of the mountain. We coasted downhill sixty miles one day."

"Now that," said Dortha, "I can understand."

"The Swiss roads are superb for cycling," said Bill, helping himself to another quart of mussels. "And the scenery beggars description. I've never been so impressed by anything in my life as I was by the view of Mont Blanc. Almost a religious experience. Next time I come to the continent I'm going to forget the rest of Europe. Spend all my time in Switzerland. It's off-season in the summertime, and we stayed at beautiful ski lodges and hostels that are out of this world. For a pittance."

I looked at the slender, muscular young man. "I'd say it was a pretty good way to stay in shape. At least it seems to work for you."

"No better way. We got so we could average a hundred kilometers a day without puffing. Our biggest day was a hundred miles. Doesn't sound like much, but it was mostly uphill."

I looked at the wife. "Did you hear that, dear?"

"I heard. The only way you're going to get me to do a hundred miles uphill is in a Mercedes Benz."

"You can see I'm not without my albatross," I said.

Bill grinned. "My girl friend was the same way at first. Now she can ride circles around me."

"You ridden much in France?" I asked.

"Quite a bit. Parts of France are great for cycling."

"How about the western part? Around Brest?"

"Ideal. You thinking of going there?"

"Not sure. We've been thinking about meeting up with a tour of the International Bicycle Touring Society. They're touring Brittany and the Loire. Thought we might join them for a while. Just to get the taste of cycling in a group."

"Tours definitely have their place. And the IBTS gangs have a ball. But if you're going to do serious, long-range bike touring, the fewer in a group the better." He chuckled. "I met up with a cycle tourist from Amsterdam. He said he started out with three buddies. By the end of the first week they had split up into three different groups."

"Maybe someone should have told them about Right Guard," said the wife.

Bill grinned. "No, nothing like that. They all wanted to set their own pace. That's very important, if you really want to get serious about long-distance cycling."

"We haven't wanted to get that serious," I said. "I'm of the opinion that if you take a sport too seriously, you start squeezing out a lot of the fun. We spend more time nosing around and taking coffee breaks—though we did click off close to sixty miles the other day. I've almost recovered from my coronary."

"That's the way to go. Set your own pace. Enjoy. It just so happens my pace can cover a fair amount of geography."

"Maybe we'll get to that stage. But right now we're taking our time and thoroughly enjoying the whole ridiculous project. When we get behind schedule, or when the weather's bad, we just throw our bikes on the train. Thank God for cheap rail transportation."

"It's a boon, all right. Thinking of taking in Great Britain?"

"We've thought about it," I said. "How is it for biking?"

"Well, if you do it right, and work out your routes with the British Cycle Federation—that's sort of a Triple A for cyclists —it can be very enjoyable. Plus, we Yanks don't have too big a language problem, which is a big help. But if you just go over on your own, like we did, it can be a bit hectic. We didn't have a bicycle route mapped out, and just tried cycling the back roads. This proved uncomfortable, especially in the southern part of England. Some British lorries are forbidden to use the freeways, and have to travel the back roads. We spent one whole weekend inhaling truck fumes. Not the best way to go. Plus the fact the British railroads are a bit stuffy about carrying bikes. They charged us half our passenger fare on the ferry over, just to haul them."

"No kidding? So your advice is to skip the British Isles?"

"Only if you're pressed for time. If you have a limited time budget, I think you'll reap far more cycling rewards on the continent. Switzerland is my favorite, as I told you, but the part of the country you've just biked through is also pretty hard to beat. Holland, being so flat, is really great."

"And Scandinavia," added Dortha.

"You bet. Superb."

We both took a shine to this ingratiating young man, and we spent a long lunch swapping lies and sharing cycling adventures. After two hours we could barely see each other over the mountain of mussel shells. I finally had to push back from the table and throw in the sponge. "Before you leave, Bill," I said, "you'd better have just a few more mussels."

He looked thoughtful for a moment. "Well, I *am* cycling to Liège tomorrow. Maybe just a small bushel. For the road."

My periphery of World War Two participation had not

included the northern coast of France. Ever since reading Winston Churchill's splendid account of the evacuation of Dunkerque, I had harbored a dream of someday visiting the Opal Coast with its string of lovely beaches that faced England. It was our intention, therefore, to cycle west through Belgium until we hit the coast, then bike down the coast, through Dunkerque, to Calais.

We rendezvoused with our party at the train station the next morning. Betty Jo and her girl friend had parted from the group, leaving Erik Swenson and the family to carry on.

The day was beset with problems before we even got under way. First, the weather went on a cantankerous binge, clouding up and pelting us with large drops of rain. A hasty huddle dictated we should head west, out of the rain, on the train. We would head for Bruges, Belgium, taking a long jump at one leap, which would give us plenty of time to cycle down the coast of northern France. This decided, we hit another snag. Brussels, being serviced by three train stations, required transporting our bikes from the Middi Station, where we had arrived, to an outlying station which offered the train to Bruges.

This was accomplished with no little difficulty—retrieving the bikes, riding through the rain and downtown traffic to the outlying station, then trying to negotiate the bikes up escalators leading to the loading platform. This unique problem was handily solved by Erik, who simply picked a bike up in each hand and raced up the escalator. A formidable chore, as the only escalator in operation was going down. I was beginning to cheerfully abide this young ton of muscle.

We checked all the bikes with the baggageman—including Erik's black gargantuan single-speed, which resembled the Eiffel Tower with wheels. Then we found a comfortable compartment on the train and whistled through the damp but beautiful Belgian countryside to Bruges.

We all agreed Bruges was far more appealing than Brussels. It is a medieval walled town, surrounded by water, with four of its seven gates still standing. Its miraculous survival is a historical accident: the river linking it with the North Sea silted up in the fifteenth century when it was a prosperous international port, leaving it high, dry, and invulnerable.

When we arrived at the Bruges depot, the nasty weather had moved out to make way for a magnificent afternoon. As we biked through the narrow, winding, Gothic streets hung with huge tapestries, I felt compelled to rattle over the cobblestones at breakneck speed on my spoked steed, and challenge to a jousting match the first mounted cyclist I saw. A cooler head prevailed, however, and we spent a very pleasant afternoon visiting the town square—not as spectacular as the one in Brussels, but every bit as interesting, with its magnificent Chapel of the Holy Blood and the Church of our Lady, where we were truly awed by Michelangelo's Virgin and Child.

We checked in at a small hotel right on the square, a retiring, low-beamed shelter with a name like a sneeze; the men took one room, the women another. Although the women's room was moderately priced, the room for the three men was suspiciously inexpensive. The reasons for its modest lease began to unfold in stages. The first stage became evident when we checked into the room. It was on the top floor, obviously a renovated attic sandwiched into the gabled roof. The ceiling was an inverted V, high in the center and meeting the floor on both sides. Crossing the room lengthwise presented little problem if one were a depressed midget wearing thin-soled socks. Crossing from left to right, however, required the delicate progress of an inchworm. A particular dilemma for Erik, who was eventually reduced to crawling around on his hands and knees after cracking two beams with his head and threatening to collapse the whole building.

Taking it all in good spirits, we washed up and adjourned

to a local restaurant renowned for its mussels—the steaming, butter-dipped mollusk I couldn't seem to get enough of—and after wading through a hogshead of the delicacies, we staggered back to our rooms, undulating like bivalves. We prepared for bed, brushing our teeth on our hands and knees at a sink improvidently placed in the corner of the room, and squeezed into our beds. Things went swimmingly until eleven o'clock sharp. Then another reason for the room's niggardly rental became manifest.

At first we thought it was an earthquake. The first reverberation cascaded Scott out of bed and bolted Erik upright in his, his head connecting with a beam which sent secondary tremors throughout the building. I, too stunned to move, stared wild-eyed at the ceiling, counting the seconds until it would descend upon me. And then the noise assumed some sort of pattern. It took a full minute to realize a carillon of gargantuan bells was playing—of all things—"Auld Lang Syne." Furthermore, the bell steeple, if not in our room, was certainly not more than twenty feet away. We listened, our heads vibrating with every gong, through a complete stanza of the farewell song. And then it quit.

When our skulls quit twanging and our eyes slowly returned to a fuzzy focus, we found the source of our traumas was the Watch Tower, located directly across the street. Its biggest brass bonger was precisely at eye level.

Not content with the first fusillade that reduced our aural acuity to that of a wombat, the tower followed up with attacks every fifteen minutes throughout the night, tolling the quarter hour. This unfortunate experience prompted me to vow: first, even if a hotel room costs five dollars a night, to pay it; second, I never again will enjoy New Year's Eve. To this day, even the mention of "Auld Lang Syne" or Guy Lombardo sends shock waves reverberating through my skull and my nerves to twanging like banjo strings.

As if to make up for our sleepless night, the sun came out the next morning in all its glory, and with Erik's help we hit the road before Holly stopped yawning. It was an easy ride through the walled city, and we hit an excellent bike trail on our way to Ostend.

We must have presented an incongruous picture. Diminutive Holly, effortlessly stroking along on her Peugeot beside the big Swede whose shoulders blanked the horizon; he pumping the pedals of his weird-looking machine, knees nearly meeting chin with every revolution.

Scott came next, cranking along vacuously, his disposition glum, his thoughts undoubtedly on the mysterious vagaries of women—particularly one brunette who apparently would rather go railroading with another girl than cycling with him.

Then came Dortha, now mistress of her volatile steed, pedaling along as pretty as you please, her bicycle and she functioning as one, the pedals and whirling wheels merely an extension of her limbs.

Then came old Ish, plodding along, the smoke from a good Dutch cigar trailing behind like the stack belchings of an old locomotive.

No longer did we feel like amateurs. Confident on our machines, flabby muscles firming up, our wind building, even the last pains of the dreaded bicycleseatus having disappeared —we began to ride like professionals. As one eventually does with practice, no longer did we boot the pedals in a knee-jerking series of thrusts; rather we were developing the smooth, gliding, second-nature rotary motion of the experienced rider. We were even giving serious thought to getting toestraps for our pedals—the hallmark of the serious cyclist. In short, we were getting into condition and enjoying it immensely. It was no longer a mystery why the new cyclemania was gripping the world. Indeed, the conundrum was how did a gas-eating, smog-belching, natural-resource-exhausting, four-wheeled engine of destruction known as the automobile—that chalks up more American fatalities every year than did the whole Vietnam War—ever become so firmly entrenched? There isn't a privately owned car in China, a country of 800 million people, and they get along famously on bicycles. So it's not a question of indispensability.

It was high time the two-wheeler came back into its own. And I, for one, was going to do what I could to speed its progress. I flexed my gluteus maximus. Maybe it was about time someone besides the French won the *Tour de France*. And didn't they have bicycle racing in the Olympics?

My ruminations were interrupted by the approach of Ostend. We cycled through the attractive resort city, had coffee at a sidewalk café, and then spun off to the beach. Ostend is the largest of Belgium's coastal communities, resplendent with a beautiful casino, thermal baths (where the water and the mud of the sea are brought to bear on nervous and respiratory afflictions and illnesses of the bones and joints), golf courses, and a famous racetrack. Forty-three miles of beautiful beaches provide superb wetting and warming facilities for the Belgian populace.

Reaching the beach road we stopped for a moment, smitten by the splendor of the sun-drenched coastline. A broad promenade lined the beach in both directions from Ostend, as far as the eye could see. The late summer weather had discouraged most of the tourists, considerably thinning the ranks of the less hardy; but the promenade was still alive with thick-blooded sun worshippers who strolled the boardwalk, or pushed baby carriages, or rode electric carts, or walked leashed dogs, or just sat on the benches along the avenue absorbing the sun.

I held up a moistened forefinger to find we had a slight tail wind (I adopted this method of testing the wind in lieu of holding up a handkerchief, since the time near Breda when I fluttered my bandanna to find I had not only a following wind, but a following Frenchman of dubious gender who shadowed me for three miles before I could shake him) and we shoved off down the promenade.

Cycling was permitted on the paved boardwalk, and we headed down the beach for what was to be one of the most enjoyable and interesting legs of our journey. Gliding along at an effortless pace through the strollers and baby carriages, we noted the gentle waves lapping up the fine sand to froth the seawall on our right and Europe's largest modern casino on our left, with its gambling rooms decorated with frescoes by Delvaux. We sailed by modern high-rise apartment buildings —some with exotic and faraway names like Hollywood Hills, Florida Arms, Miami Palms, and Saratoga Spa. Then leaving behind the toy sellers, the refreshment stands, and the congestion of the Belgian Coast's queen of watering places, we traded the high-rise apartments for Sahara-like sand dunes; the beach cabanas and sun umbrellas for a vast expanse of desolate, unspoiled beach.

Exhilarated by the tangy sea air and the stunning, simplistic beauty of sea, sand, and sailcloth, we traversed the ten kilometers to Middelkerke without realizing we had energized a muscle. Here, the troops could no longer endure the heady seduction of waves and sand, and I was issued an ultimatum. During a stop for a tea break I was informed by Scott, the self-imposed head of the mutiny party, that we were going to anchor here for the night and allow the party to have shore leave and a swim in the ocean.

A man who can accept defeat gracefully when it is inevitable, I knuckled under. While the mutineers changed into swim togs at a public swimming pool carved out of the beach, Dortha watched the bikes and I started scouting for a room for the night.

Middelkerke is a lovely seacoast town that caters to the seagoing public with its own casino and ten-kilometer seawall promenade. It boasts an excellent asphalt trail through its rolling sand dunes, a nearby airport that services flights between Belgium and Great Britain, and a church with a miraculous cross discovered on the beach several centuries ago. It is woefully lacking, however, in hotels that are open in the middle of September. It doesn't possess the late-season grandeur of neighboring Ostend, and this time of year sees the fickle tourist seeking his holiday in climes farther south. Leaving the Middelkerke resort hotel owners to shutter up their windows and follow suit.

It was by pure luck I obtained accommodations for my brood at a nice hotel called the Terminus, only half a block from the ocean. Having found an open bar off the boardwalk, I went in to inquire about local facilities that might be open. It so happened the bartender spoke no English, but a fellow sitting at the bar did, and in addition to his linguistic ability, he also happened to possess the Terminus Hotel. Although his hotel was empty, as he was in the process of securing it for the winter, he allowed he might take in four aliens providing we could cope with the fact the heat had been turned off. Suggesting a nightly rate for the five of us I couldn't refuse had it been a basement in a leaky igloo, we struck a fast deal.

"*Godvecdomme!*" he exclaimed, when he saw five bicycles invading the bar of his hotel. He recovered quickly, however, to become the perfect host, even opening the bar for me. And for the first time in our lives we had our pick of any room in a hotel. We settled on two facing the ocean, then proceeded to liquidate the entire inventory of a nearby restaurant, whose owner, fortunately, was in the throes of closing it anyway. Appetites whetted by cycling, honed by coldwater swimming, then stropped by lots of energetic shivering produced a tableclothed wasteland of spent chicken carcasses, lamb legs, T-bones and seashells not equaled since the invasion of the Mormon crickets.

We struggled up the stairs of the silent hotel to dive immediately under warm comforters and thus evade the chilling drafts of the unheated hotel. With the setting of the sun it had become colder than a marble cutter's tutu.

The sandman made an early appearance, overtured by the rattle of contented snoring and orchestrated by loud gurglings and rumblings of draining hotel plumbing.

12

"Shoot at the Tires of a Bicycle Thief?"

IT took considerable doing the next morning to get everyone awake, but once accomplished, the frosty air in the hotel prompted a new speed record for racing from warm sheets to bike saddle. The sun, rising about the same time we did, soon had adrenalin pumping, chilblains thawed, and dispositions rosy. It was another magnificent day for cycling, the breeze at our back, and just cool enough to make the warm sun feel good. We whistled along the beach promenade until we found a small café open. After breakfast we cut inland with the road to bridge the Yser River, then through wooded dune and bird reserves to Nieuwpoort. And a step back into history.

Totally destroyed in the First World War, Nieuwpoort refused to die and boomeranged back to life, rebuilding in a harmonious style. We passed peasants strolling among the Flemish houses, visited the ruins of the Templar's Tower and the Church of St. Lawrence, which latter was ravaged by the English during the siege of 1383. We took time to find Duynenhuys, the house in the dunes where Archduke Albert and Archduchess

Isabella once lived; then we tracked down the bust of Geeraert the lockkeeper, a temptestuous gent who didn't like the idea of having his country invaded, so in 1914 he spoiled the plans of the Central Powers by simply opening the gates and flooding the plain of Yser. A man who certainly knew how to cool a battle.

We again picked up the beach road to wend through Oostduinkerke-on-Sea, a resort with the most picturesque dunes on the Belgian Coast, which were occupied by old fisherfolk houses. Here, on a spectacular beach that stretches as far as five hundred meters at low tide, we stopped to wonder at men on horseback, dragging nets through the surf. We were told they were shrimp fishermen, seining for the delectable crustaceans.

Nearing De Panne, where the beach extends without interruption for over thirty kilometers, we saw why the stirring sport of sand-yachting had originated here. We came upon one of these three-wheeled sand boats that was just spreading its sail to capture the breeze. As it started to roll along the broad expanse of beach, Erik waved at the land yachtsman. He made the mistake of waving back.

This was a signal for a race. Erik accelerated his clumsy bicycle, spurting ahead of the sand yacht. Then the wind began to bellow the sails of the sand boat, it started picking up speed, and the race was on. Erik put his heart and soul into it, his feet churning like a road runner's. For a short time it was nip and tuck. If the Swede had had a racing bike instead of his two-wheeled tank between his powerful legs, it might have been close. But as it was, he was no match for the sail cycle, which could attain speeds of eighty miles an hour. With its canvas spread to its fullest, the skipper nonchalantly waved as he pulled ahead of the sweating Swede.

Erik panted to a stop, and we all gathered around the good-natured giant, congratulating him on coming in second.

Holly put the capper on with a kiss on the cheek. This almost inspired the man to reengage his opponent, and it took all of us to stop him.

De Panne was the last bastion, the final plot of Belgian territory never overrun by the enemy in World War I. Today, in the flourishing resort town, moving vestiges remain to prod the memory of those dramatic times. The stirring British War Cemetery is here, as is the crypt of Our Lady of Fatima. However, it was the sea-bicycling, the sand-yachting clubs, and the roller-skating on the seafront that commanded the interest of the younger set.

As we cycled along the boardwalk, dodging roller skaters, pedestrians, and perambulators, we decreed this would be a good place to have lunch. The wind had kicked up a bit, and preferring our sandwiches sans sand, we sought refuge behind the glass enclosure that surrounded a public heated swimming pool situated on the promenade. We were just biting into our lunch when the most unforgettable happening on the trip occurred.

I was handing Dortha a glass of milk when I saw her suddenly freeze, eyes bugging, her sandwich halfway to her mouth. She was staring over the cement wall that held the glass enclosure, at the spot where our bikes were parked. I followed her gaze. And then my eyes bugged.

"I don't believe it," she said. "*Look!*"

I was looking. I was seeing a young man in a black leather jacket bending over Dortha's bicycle. His eyes were darting around furtively, obviously not seeing us behind the salt-sprayed glass of the pool enclosure. Then he straightened up enough so we could see he was trying to remove a white object from the back rack of Dortha's bicycle. Then I recognized it as Dortha's purse. "My God!" I gasped. "Dortha, *he's stealing your purse!*" I leaped to my feet.

The sudden commotion behind the opaque glass caught

the thief's eye. He hesitated for a second, trying to free the straps of the purse wrapped around the rack. Unable to get them untangled, he decided to take it—bicycle and all. This was not a difficult feat, since we had parked the bikes where we could keep an eye on them—and left them unlocked.

He started running with the bicycle. Gathering speed he threw himself awkwardly onto the seat. He started weaving uncertainly through the crowd, trying to master the unaccustomed ten-speed.

"Let's get him!" I yelled. *"He's got Dortha's purse!"*

"And my bicycle," added Dortha.

Spraying sand, I sprinted toward my bike. Right on my heels were Scott and Erik. *"You girls stay here,"* I threw back over my shoulder. *"The thief might be dangerous."*

"Holly, stay here," barked Dortha, right behind us. *"The thief might be dangerous."*

Leapfrogging over the rear wheel and onto my seat, I was the first off on a running start. Scott was right behind me. Erik, taking a little longer to get his big mass in motion, was coming up fast. Unbeknownst to me, Dortha had commandeered Holly's bike and was bringing up the rear. Thus started the wildest, wooliest chase in the annals of unorganized crime.

The thief had made several errors in judgment. Not the least of which was wearing a black jacket that was easily spotted in the crowd. And hijacking a ten-speed bicycle without first having been introduced to its idiosyncrasies wasn't too bright. He was wobbling through traffic, near-missing passersby as he struggled desperately with the shift levers trying to lure them into high speed. For this reason we were actually gaining on him at first. Then, finally fumbling the gears into top speed, he took off like a shot, his churning adrenalin providing a JATO boost.

Seeing a bicycling gendarme up ahead, my spirits soared. I swung abreast of him. *"Bicycle thief,"* I yelled, pointing ahead at the fleeing figure. *"Catch him!"*

"*Shoot at his tires,*" yelled Scott.

Then my spirits plummeted as I saw the obesity of the patrolman. Obviously far more at home corralling plates of pasta than pedaling purloiners, he waved jovially as we sped by.

If we were to apprehend the culprit, it would now be up to Scott, Erik, and myself.

Weaving through promenading strollers, baby carriages, and mechanized carts, it was a sporty course. Scott shot on ahead, his derriere pointing at the sky, his eyes at handlebar level. He was starting to gain on the purse snatcher when a sad thing happened. A young lady in a short-skirted skater's outfit suddenly materialized ahead, lazily practicing figure eights on roller skates. Scott clanged his bell. This startled the young lady, who immediately started skating as fast as she could to get out of his way. She was trying to outguess his intentions, he hers. The inevitable happened.

I shut my eyes. When I found the courage to reopen them, Scott was spinning along with a very surprised figure skater straddling his handlebars, holding on for dear life. This added weight reduced his speed, and he couldn't see around the head blocking his field of vision. There was a squeal of rubber. His wild flight was safely arrested, but not, alas, before coming into contact with a balloon seller. I glanced back just long enough to see a score of multicolored balloons lifting into the sky, marking a trio of tangled torsos.

It was now up to Erik and me.

And Erik was having trouble getting any speed out of his ponderous, low-geared machine. The distance between us and the thief was rapidly increasing. Pumping along side by side, we parted to bracket a little lady in a wheelchair, then rejoined, racing along neck and neck. "*I got an idea, Colonel,*" he yelled. "*We'll never catch him this way.*"

I shot him a look. "*What's your idea?*"

Instead of answering, he was staring out toward the beach.

Suddenly he peeled off toward the seawall. I yelled at him. As he reached the edge, he launched off the high embankment into space. Astonished, I watched him sail through the air, then disappear from sight toward the sand below. "The kid's ripped a hole in his marble bag," I muttered, renewing my efforts to force more speed from my bicycle.

It was now up to me.

Slitting my eyes against the wind, I could still make out the fugitive up ahead. He was pedaling furiously. Glancing back to see he was still being pursued, he redoubled his efforts. With the resort center now behind us, the crowd had thinned to nothing but a few fishermen. And looking up ahead I could see the paved boardwalk itself was coming to an end. In the distance it seemed to slope down and merge with the beach.

I was in trouble. Maybe I could keep up with my quarry as long as we were on bikes, thanks to my conditioning. But if we hit soft sand, I was dead. The thief would abandon the bike, rip off Dortha's purse, and a half-century-old poop would have no hopes of keeping up with a young man through the sand dunes on foot. And there went the wife's wallet, passport, credit cards—everything.

I groaned as I stared up ahead. The promenade was ending in a steep incline that led to the beach. The culprit sailed down the incline, pedaling with all his might, then swooshed into the soft sand. His bike came to an abrupt halt, sending him tumbling. He quickly picked himself up and grabbed the purse. Then making a gesture at me that should not be described in a book of propriety, he turned toward the dunes, a triumphant look on his face.

It was precisely at this moment I discovered Erik Swenson hadn't lost all his marbles after all.

He was very easy to recognize in the seat of the sand yacht, as his shoulders were nearly a match for the sail. There was a cloud of displaced sand as the craft skidded directly in front of a very surprised purse snatcher. Not completely at home in a sailboat that operated on land, Erik was not successful in keeping it from capsizing as he skidded to a halt. An axled wheel whipped up to replace the position normally enjoyed by the sail, flinging its occupant in a huge, rolling snowball to land at the feet of the dumbfounded fugitive. And then the young thief was no longer dumbfounded, he was apoplectic as the snowball in front of him changed into a wall of muscle, which at the moment was hoisting him up by the collar while his churning feet displaced nothing but air a good distance above the ground.

I arrived upon the scene to hit the sand at a speed of approximately Mach one. There ensued a graceful, arcing handstand over the handlebars, which culminated in a face-down landing in the grit. I no sooner hit than I found myself being raised aloft in Erik's other hand, spitting and wiping sand from my eyes.

My vision cleared in time to see Scott roaring down the chute like Strawberry Roan. Then his front wheel dug in, bucking him out of the saddle in the most perfectly executed half gainer to date. He was netted by the sail of the land yacht.

Then a loud, piercing *"Yyiiiiiiiikes"* commanded our attention. Here came Dortha, her big eyes suddenly platter-size as she saw what she was getting into. Rocketing down the slope, her wheels hit the beach, ground to a halt, and catapulted her neatly over the handlebars. I spun sand trying to get to her, but was too late. Erik beat me to the interception, plucking her out of the sky as she flew by, as calmly as O. J. Simpson might snag a bullet pass behind the goal line.

And then came the gendarme, pedaling along as furiously as his midsection handicap allowed, being egged on by Holly from her side-saddle position on the bar of his bike. Too late to avoid the booby trap, he hit the incline and slammed on the brakes. This triggered a precise, 360-degree turn as he slithered down the ramp, miraculously keeping upright, only to hit the sand at the bottom. There was a loud Belgian *"Ooooomph"* as he parted company with his bike. This was followed by an even louder Belgian *"Ooooomph"* as Holly landed on top of him.

It took fully five minutes of poking through the bodies to make a head count and ascertain that everyone had escaped the ridiculous melee without serious injury. The worst damage of all seemed to have been suffered by Dortha's potted plant. It had received a severe shock, being divorced, as it was, from its pot. Dortha replaced it in its container, clucking and sympathizing.

Slowly piecing the picture together, it appeared that Erik, searching for some conveyance that could outrun his bicycle, had noticed the sand yacht just starting up on the beach behind the seawall. It was this observation that prompted his high-flying circus act over the seawall. He had lit in the sand, sans bicycle, but on pumping legs that propelled him over to the accelerating sand yacht. Not taking time to explain, he commandeered the vehicle by the expedient of replacing the shanks of the skipper with those of his own. The rest we had witnessed.

It took an hour or so to replace a few divots. The Belgian owner of the sand yacht appeared on the scene in a highly turbulent state, still digging sand out of his eye from his unseemly dislocation. Finding the reason for the abduction—not to mention the shoulder width of the abductor—he was quickly mollified, and went on his way with a crisp bill in his pocket and a new reverence for his wind-blown thief-chaser.

The gendarme proved a bit harder to conciliate. Once we got his breathing apparatus resuming normal function, it was apparent someone would have to hang for all the indignities heaped upon the long arm of the law. It was Holly, using the same beguiling ways she had used to convince him to give chase in the first place, that finally simmered him down to rationality.

And this posed a problem, as Dortha took one look at the thief trembling in the grasp of Erik's hamlike fist and decided she didn't want to press charges. "He's so young," she said, casting her calf eyes at me. "He must be Holly's age. And he looks so undernourished."

"For anyone suffering from malnutrition," I said, "he can sure as hell ride a bike."

"Honey, let me handle this." Interpreting my grunt as a sign of approval, she marched the young man over and sat him down on a dune bank.

The schoolteacher in her surfacing, there were five minutes of finger-shaking in the face. Serious tones alternated with sympathy-provoking gestures as she showed him the condition of her plant. Then more stern, eye-flashing pronouncements. The words were uncomprehensible to the youth, but there was no confusion about the morality lecture being intoned. From the perspiration beads gathering on the lad's brow, it was obvious the dire pronouncements of a judge would have been vastly preferred.

Finishing, she gave him a little hug of forgiveness. Then she joined us. "I'm sure he'll never do that again. Andy, give me some money. I want to give it to this young man."

I looked at her, blinking audibly. "I had a nasty fall. I'm not hearing right, am I?"

"You heard me. Give me some money for this boy."

"You are out of your gourd! This kid steals your purse and your bicycle. And you want to *reward* him?"

"Not reward. Salvage. Anoint my palm."

"Definitely not. I'm not paying anyone to give me a heart attack."

"That's not a Christian attitude."

"Maybe not, Billy Graham, but if you want him to have some money so badly, *you* give him some. I refuse to reward thievery. Take some out of your purse he tried to steal."

"There's no money in my purse."

"I beg your pardon?"

"I carry all my money and valuables in my jacket." She unzipped a pocket and produced her wallet. "See? There's nothing of value in my purse. Some cheese, a few teabags, a flashlight, corkscrew, several cute little pine cones from Denmark,"—she wrinkled her forehead in thought—"oh, yes, and a tablespoon of fish fertilizer. You know, for the plant, and—"

Naturally, I ended up paying the lad a few francs for going to all the trouble of stealing Dortha's bicycle. And with the policeman finally placated, we shook the sand from our machines and continued on to Dunkerque, passing through customs into France.

Belgium should be appreciated, as it performs an easy transition between Holland and France, combining some of the features of both. To go from sparkling clean Holland smack into the rural areas of France would be entirely too much of a shock. Not that rural France isn't interesting. But one has to get used to decaying farmhouses, pigs in the front yard, and clotheslines that serve as chicken roosts.

We stopped to investigate the old fortifications along the coast—concrete pillboxes and gun emplacements that smelled of urine and mold—crumbling testimonials to man's follies dating back to the beginning of the social order. And then the wagon master made a wrong turn, and we ended up on bustling Highway N-40 for the last ten kilometers to Dunkerque. We had to share the shoulder of the road with speeding cars and thundering trucks that tended either to blow us off the road or suck us along in their vacuum. We were acutely beginning to miss the cycle paths and priorities we had enjoyed in the lowland countries.

Exhaling exhaust fumes, we coughed into Dunkerque. We finally located the tourist office, and were disappointed by the reception of a lachrymose Frenchman who informed us there were no rooms to be had in the whole city; no trains out of Dunkerque, only motor buses which would not accept bicycles; no cycling roads leading out of the city; and the nearest accommodations to be had were in Calais, forty kilometers down the coast. Tired, dirty, and frustrated, I set out on foot to find a place to sleep.

I found two rooms at the first hotel I checked, further adding fuel to my belief that the French tourist office had it in for Americans. Discussing the situation with the clerk at the hotel, he put my mind at ease, saying the Dunkerque tourist office treated everybody the same way—badly. Someday they would have to do something about it.

To add ignominy to the situation, it developed that the hotel's only shower was out of commission—a malady not too uncommon in small French hotels. Our room did provide, however, the first portable bidet we had seen. This necessitated an improvisation that may well go down in history. It's tough taking a bath in a bidet. Especially if one has long legs. And this provided a particular dilemma to wide-beamed Erik, who promptly got stuck, and wore the contraption around the room like a porcelain bustle, cursing and complaining in Swedish, until Scott and I finally managed to extract him with generous ladlings of soapsuds. It was a moment not without its humor. Even Scott went into hysterics.

We ate dinner at a typical small French restaurant, recommended by the hotel, where we were assured of excellent cuisine at a reasonable price. It was typically French; the cuisine was excellent, and we were hit with a bill that would have stag-

gered Rockefeller. I was beginning to see why the British went
to such extremes to evacuate Dunkerque. With treatment like
this, I couldn't wait to evacuate four Americans and one Swede.

We decamped early the next morning. Determined not to
spend the day inhaling the noxious fumes of traffic on busy
N-40 all the way to Calais, I got a rare brainstorm and looked
up the local French Automobile Club. Flashing my triple A
card, I expected the usual runaround. To my surprise, I received the attention of a knowledgeable Frenchman, who
knocked himself out charting the best bicycle route to Calais.

Armed with a detailed map and renewed faith in our
fellow Frenchman, we backroaded along peaceful, sparsely
trafficked streets all the way to Loon-Plage. Here I made the
mistake of stopping the convoy to check my map.

As Erik, Scott, and I were studying the situation, along
came a French motorcyclist. Complete with leather jacket, put-
tees, scarf, and leather helmet with goggles, yet, I was sure
he was a French messenger who had been holed up in some
revetment since World War I, and was now on his way to
General La Follette with a secret dispatch. He passed us, then
noting we were puzzling over a map, he braked to a stop.
He turned around and approached. *"Où allez-vous?"* he asked.

While I tried to figure out what he said, Dortha replied.
"Calais."

"Ah, oui. Calais." His pencil moustache made a V for
Victory sign. *"Suivez-moi."*

I looked at Dortha. "He said follow me," she said.

Gunning his motorcycle around, he started down the road,
beckoning with his arm. We put the spurs to our steeds and
followed.

It took some doing to keep up. But for a good three kilometers we kept him in sight, our pedals a blur. At last he pulled

up to a stop sign. "Calais," he said, pointing down the road that intersected the one we were on.

"*Merci beaucoup,*" I said. "And good luck with the war."

"*Ce n'est rien,*" he replied, smiling and waving. Then he spun around and headed back in the direction from which we had just come.

"Well," panted Dortha. "Wasn't that nice of that young man? Going out of his way like that."

"Very nice," I said. I looked down the road to which we had been directed. A covey of trucks was advancing. I checked my map. We were back on good old congested, diesel-fumed Highway N-40!

We wallowed in truck smog the seven kilometers to Gravelines, where at last we were able to peel off onto a back road. From here on it became a pleasant, leisurely trip through the French countryside. We lunched in a peaceful meadow, and while the brood took a short nap in the sun, I rode alone along a small road leading to the beach.

I sat down on a sand dune and allowed my mind's eye to turn back the clock thirty years to World War II and the time when this beach had been full of Allied soldiers, driven to the very brink of catastrophe by German troops. I could see the plucky Englishmen shoving off from Britain's coastline to cross the treacherous channel, manning anything that floated—from yachts to rowboats—to evacuate more than 350,000 Allied troops. It was a daring, marvelous feat, unequaled in history.

My nostalgic mood eventually sated, I returned to the meadow. Assembling the group, we finished the pleasant journey to Calais.

We were as delighted with Calais as we had been disappointed with Dunkerque. A lively, bright, with-it city—called the key to France and its most important passenger port—it is the nearest continental town to Great Britain. From here the channel can be crossed in thirty minutes, thanks to the new hovercraft services, to completely change country and scenery. Situated between the hills of the Boulogne area and the plains of Flanders, Calais blends the beauty of its countryside with the excitement of the sea. It presented a very favorable impression, for which we were glad.

For here we had to make a command decision.

The young adults had several times mentioned how nice it would be to take off on their own for awhile, biking and hosteling it. Not that they weren't having a good time with the old poops, they hastily added. They were. But they felt it would be a broadening experience to spend some time with their own peer group. To really round out the trip. Dortha and I discussed it, and had agreed it would be great for the offspring to meet Europeans of their own age. We had decided to reserve a decision until reaching Calais. This would give us a chance to assess the young Swede, to find out if he would be a suitable companion for our daughter; and to find out the plans of Betty Jo, who was to meet us in Calais.

Properly settled in a nice hotel, the youngsters were sent on missions: Holly and Erik to get the mail—Calais being one of our pickup points—and Scott to the local automobile club in search of cycling maps of the area.

It was a long-faced Holly who returned first, bearing news that Betty Jo would not be meeting us in Calais. She and her girl friend had elected to see England first, adding that perhaps she and Scott could join up later on. This was bad news, indeed, for Scott's morale had never really gotten off its knees since we left Brussels. This message was certain to throw him into deeper fits of depression.

Later, alone in the room, Dortha and I were discussing the best way to break the news to Scott, when he returned from the auto club. Bursting into the room, he did several *entrechats* that would have awed Nijinsky, and tossed an armful of maps into my lap. "Mission accomplished, sir," he said. "And how." Surprised by this display of elevated spirits, I was on the verge of requesting an explanation when he said, "I'd like to have you meet someone."

"We'd like to meet someone," said Dortha, puzzled.

"Then I shall bring her in." Scott went to the open door, bowed grandly, and made a sweeping motion with his arm. "Please come into the lair of my mater and pater."

In walked one of the loveliest young ladies I have ever seen. Even a hiker's backpack slung over one shoulder did not detract from a slender, well-proportioned figure. Long, lustrous black hair escaped from a saucy beret to frame a high-cheekboned model's face. A pair of big, warm-brown eyes swept the room. "May I present Miss Yvonne Renoir," said Scott. "Yvonne, my mother and father."

Dortha acknowledged the introduction, and I rose to accept the slender hand presented to me. I noticed Yvonne's eyes seemed to have a smile of their own, indifferent to what the rest of her face was doing. "Very happy to meet you, Miss Renoir."

"My pleasure, Monsieur Anderson." Her voice matched her eyes.

"You won't believe this," said Scott, "but Yvonne is on a holiday. She's touring the country. We met at the auto club over a map of the Corniche de la Côte d'Opale."

"How interesting," said Dortha.

"I thought so," said Scott. "That's where Yvonne's planning to hike. Did you know this area is also great for cycling? Many natural sites such as the Cap Blanc-Nez, from which can be seen the magnificent sweep of the Bay of Wissant, and the Cap Gris-Nez, from which swimmers leave to cross the channel, and—"

"No," I said. "I didn't know that."

I did know that Scott's jubilant mood might help absorb the shock of the news from Betty Jo. Taking advantage of an animated conversation between Dortha and Yvonne, I took him aside. "I've got a bit of bad news," I said.

"Lay it on me, Pop."

"It's about Betty Jo. She's not going to meet us here."

"Oh? Betty Jo who?"

Needless to say, that ended that conversation.

And so the decision was made the following morning.

During dinner the night before, Yvonne had seemed as sweet as she was pretty and intelligent. She was a French governess who had a job caring for the children of a wealthy family in Calais, and was just starting her two weeks' vacation. It so happened she loved cycling more than any sport in the world, and would give anything to cycle tour the French Coast. But she had not been able to afford a bicycle of her own.

It was also quite apparent she and Scott were not exactly grooming to be enemies.

The distaff and I had already made up our minds about Erik Swenson. He was a big, awkward, likable Greyhound bus, with a dry, sparkling sense of humor. We both heartily endorsed him, and if anyone could protect our little daughter in the wilds of Europe, he was the man for the job.

Dortha and I would have liked to cycle down the French Coast, to meet up with the International Bicycle Touring Society that was now touring Brittany. But it was clear that personal druthers must on occasion take the back seat to troop morale, and as Clausewitz put it, a good commander takes care of the men and horses first. Accordingly, we would turn our bikes over to the youngsters, and Dortha and I would take to the trains.

I had two weeks to go before my Eurailpass expired, the same date I had to be in New York to help launch the publication of my new book. This would give us time to visit London, which we loved; maybe Paris, which we abided; certainly Rome, before it slid into the mire of bankruptcy; and Venice, before it slid into the sea. Then we would drop by Geneva, to pay a visit to Hank Ketcham's domain in a penthouse overlooking the city, from where he ruled his private little world with the help of Dennis the Menace. From Switzerland we hoped to cruise down the Rhine River to Frankfurt.

Accordingly, that afternoon Dortha, her eyes puddling in spite of herself, bade farewell to her bike. She gave instructions on the care and feeding of her potted plant, and turned her steed over to Yvonne. I, ridiculing myself for having become so attached to a piece of well-machined steel, turned my bike over to Erik, whose ambulating Eiffel Tower had developed a bad limp since hurdling the seawall at De Panne. It had been relegated to the Calais equivalent of our Goodwill Industries.

Then Dortha took Holly aside for a private little talk having to do, I'm sure, with the evil designs of men; and I gave Scott a briefing about his new responsibilities as wagon master. I also extracted from him a promise to meet us in Frankfurt two weeks hence.

Scott's yo-yoing morale was currently hovering around the peak of Mont Blanc as he mounted his bike alongside the vivacious French girl. As we watched them shove off, Yvonne demonstrated that in addition to being proficient in five languages, she would have no problem becoming proficient in ten-speed bicycles.

Holly kissed us good-bye, then swung up on her bike, looking lark-happy and throat-lumping vulnerable next to her huge escort. Erik thanked us for everything. Dortha surprised him with a kiss, and he picked her up off the ground in a bear hug. I watched fearfully, but he tenderly replaced her, then faced me and popped to attention.

"At ease," I said, extending my hand. "I've been meaning to tell you it's not necessary to salute retired officers."

He grinned, unveiling an acre of enamel. "I know that, sir." He gripped my hand, then tucked the bike between his long shanks. Before I could massage the feeling back into my digits, the troop had whisked from view.

It was late afternoon when Dortha and I caught the ferry to Dover. We were at the ship's rail, watching the gulls wheeling in our wake as we cruised across the channel. "I'm going to miss the kids," she said.

"I hate to admit it, but I will, too."

"They'll have a marvelous time." She slipped her hand into mine. "Well, love, we did it. We old poops cycled through five countries and lived to tell about it. In retrospect, how do you rate the Great Bicycle Expedition?"

I lit a cigarette, cupping the lighter flame against the breeze. "It adds up to one of the most memorable experiences of my life. For several reasons. For one, I've been worrying about the American image overseas. Some of our carp-tongued politicos have led the American people to believe we've lost all our friends in Europe. Having just spent weeks of eyeball-to-eyeball contact with citizens of half a dozen different countries, I know this isn't true."

"I didn't know you were making a social study."

"I wasn't. Turned out to be a fringe benefit."

"It's a cinch they didn't like the Andersons for their money. Not when we drive up to small hotels on bicycles and snitch breakfast rolls for our lunch. What else about the trip turned you on? Think we've proved cycling is a good, inexpensive way to see Europe?"

I looked at her in surprise. "Don't you?"

"Definitely. But I don't think it's for everyone."

"It's not for the luxury-loving, Hilton Hotel crowd. Nor for the jet set. It's for people who want to really *live* Europe. Not just test its cocktail bars and splash in its bidets. For people who love adventure, who aren't afraid of the unknown, who don't shy from physical exercise, who . . ."

"Pretty extravagant."

"It was cheap. The days of Europe on five bucks a day exist now only in Arthur Frommer's imagination. But by cycling and staying at small hotels and pensions, we probably did it in grand style for around ten bucks a day per person. Even considering today's devaluation of the dollar." I slapped my abdomen. "And there's another fallout from the trip. Maybe it's the best one. I don't have trouble bending over to tie my shoelaces anymore."

"Me neither. I'm going to continue cycling when we get home. I've never felt better in my life."

I reached down and patted her fan. "It's a cinch you never looked better. I'll bet you've reshuffled at least five pounds."

"Ten." She stuck out her chest. "And I lost my pot. In spite of all that great food we stashed away."

"I've shed a couple spare tires."

She smiled up at me. "So you consider your mission successful, wagon master? Mission complete?"

"Not quite. But tonight, when I get you all alone in that London hotel room, you'd better oil your track shoes. Or I'll complete the mission in a blaze of glory."

She gave me a leering look. "You little dickens."

"Aint it the truth."

I was glad she was in a good mood. Maybe this was the time to bring up my new idea. My plan for our next venture. I mulled it for a moment, then decided against it. I would wait until tonight. Get her into bed, mellow with a good bottle of chablis. Then I'd fan her with the seductive aroma of my new French shaving lotion and spring it on her. How could she possibly refuse?

So instead of mentioning it now, I patted the clipping in my pocket I had torn out of the *Stars and Stripes*. The one that told about the college professor who was looking for volunteers to bicycle with him through Communist China.

Yes, it would definitely be better to bring it up later.

Instead, I put my arm around my wife's streamlined waist, and the two of us silently watched the white cliffs of Dover loom up over the starboard bow.